PRAISE FOR *THE PANAMA HAT TRAIL*

"Part reportage, part travelogue, and all pleasure; it is written with enthusiasm and wit. . . . It is filled with lively anecdotes, pungent asides, vivid scenes, and—best of all in a travel book—delightful characters."

—*Washington Post*

"Absorbing . . . a lively, entertaining exploration. Chock-full of the enthusiasm and energy of the experienced traveler. . . . *The Panama Hat Trail* is an armchair adventure that shouldn't be missed."

—*Boston Herald*

"One of the most thoughtful and engaging travel books in recent memory, a superlative job of reporting. . . . A wonderful book with a rich mixture of native and expatriate eccentrics."

—*Playboy*

"Fascinating . . . like a detective story in which one clue leads to another until the complex fabric of a society slowly reveals itself."

—*Kirkus Reviews*

"One eagerly and joyously turns the pages of this lively and vivid account. Each page is loaded with rich treasures."

—*Latin America in Books*

"Strange and wonderful characters, rich descriptions, and even richer anecdotes."

—*San Diego Tribune*

"Miller has a fine, unobtrusive, offhand way of writing. He is a good and conscientious correspondent who has produced a lively, memorable book."

—*Outsid*

T0168671

THE PANAMA HAT TRAIL

OTHER BOOKS BY TOM MILLER

Trading with the Enemy: A Yankee Travels Through Castro's Cuba
Cuba, Hot and Cold
Revenge of the Saguaro: Offbeat Travels Through America's Southwest
On the Border: Portraits of America's Southwestern Frontier
The Assassination Please Almanac

EDITOR:
*How I Learned English: 55 Accomplished Latinos Recall Lessons in
    Language and Life*
Travelers' Tales Cuba: True Stories
Writing on the Edge: A Borderlands Reader

THE PANAMA HAT TRAIL

 TOM MILLER

THE UNIVERSITY OF
ARIZONA PRESS

TUCSON

The University of Arizona Press
www.uapress.arizona.edu

Originally published in hardcover by William Morrow and Company, Inc., 1986
Published in paperback by Vintage Departures, Random House, Inc., 1988
First University of Arizona Press paperback edition, 2017

Printed in the United States of America
22 21 20 19 18 17   6 5 4 3 2 1

ISBN-13: 978-0-8165-3587-3 (paper)

Cover design by Leigh McDonald

Grateful acknowledgment is made for permission to reprint excerpts from the following: *The Donkey Inside*, by Ludwig Bemelmans. Reprinted by permission of International Creative Management, Inc. Copyright © 1927, 1938, 1940, 1941 by Ludwig Bemelmans. Copyright renewed. "Assembly Line," by B. Traven. Reprinted with permission of Scott Meredith Literary Agency, Inc. Copyright © 1966 by B. Traven. "El Sombrero de Montecristi," by Lupi. Reprinted by permission of Luis Espinosa Martinez. Copyright © 1964 by Luis Espinosa Martinez. "Juan Cuenca—Biografía del Pueblo Sombrero," by G. H. Mata. Reprinted by permission of Centro Interamericano de Artesanías y Artes Populares (CIDAP). Copyright © 1978 by G. H. Mata. "Folk Arts Thrive in a Quito Shop" and "City at the 'Middle of the World'" originally appeared in the January 16, 1983, and the January 22, 1984, issues of the *New York Times*, respectively. Copyright © 1983 and 1984 by The New York Times Company. Reprinted by permission.

Library of Congress Cataloging-in-Publication Data
Names: Miller, Tom, 1947– author.
Title: The Panama hat trail / Tom Miller.
Description: 2017 edition with new preface by author. | Tucson : The University of Arizona Press, 2017. | Includes bibliographical references and index.
Identifiers: LCCN 2017007700 | ISBN 9780816535873 (pbk. : alk. paper)
Subjects: LCSH: Ecuador—Description and travel. | Ecuador—Social life and customs. | Hat trade—Ecuador. | Miller, Tom, 1947– —Travel—Ecuador.
Classification: LCC F3716 .M55 2017 | DDC 918.6604—dc23 LC record available at https://lccn.loc.gov/2017007700

♾ This paper meets the requirements of ANSI/NISO Z39.48-1992 (Permanence of Paper).

To Val

CONTENTS

PART THREE

PART FOUR

PREFACE TO THE 2017 EDITION

If you've peeked at the introduction a page or two from here, you'll recall a passage quoting a U.S. State Department officer commenting that "Ecuador has a severe inferiority complex." When this book first came out in 1986, I had quite the opposite sensation. Reviews were wonderful, including one in the *Washington Post* that appeared just days prior to a book signing at Olsson's, a since shuttered Georgetown bookstore. Bowls of candy sat by stacks of books. My publisher sent a rep to assure a smooth event. It was a comfortably warm late summer weekday evening, and the casually dressed patrons snaked through the store practically out the door onto Wisconsin Avenue.

A slight hubbub arose as a determined-looking man in a three-piece suit maneuvered his way to the front of the line.

"Mr. Miller?" He said this more as a statement than a question.

I nodded.

He snapped his card at me. He was Mario Leon-Meneses, counselor from the Embassy of Ecuador.

"Mr. Miller, we are very concerned at your characterization of Ecuador as having a 'severe inferiority complex.'"

Then, having proven the characterization, Mr. Leon-Meneses turned on his heels and walked out.

The one product Ecuador can feel superior about is the Panama hat, whose name provokes national pride and international confusion. I'm not spoiling your reading adventure by stating that Panamas come from Ecuador, but now, even within Ecuador, there's controversy about the various styles of Panamas, their weaves, and their towns of origin.

This is the trail, very roughly, as it has been followed for well over a century: straw cutter → weekly straw market → weaver → middleman → factory finishing → exporting. In recent generations, however, many weavers have found more lucrative work, and fewer weavers means fewer hats. All this makes for a diminishing industry. "In twenty years," lamented the late Carlos Barberán who promoted and sold high-quality hats, "the weaving of the Montecristi *finos* will be all over." That was in the mid-1980s.

Montecristi Panamas are known internationally for their soft, air-tight weave and clean, honey-smooth surface. And they originate in Ecuador's coastal region of Montecristi. The finest are more art than headwear. Most Panamas, however, come from the Cuenca region high in the Andes 275 kilometers distant, where midrange hats predominate. That is, except for the very best from the Cuenca region, which are marketed as Montecristi hats. As a result, Montecristi becomes both adjective and proper noun. The confusion: a hat named for the Canton of Montecristi comes from a city called Cuenca, branded as a product of Panama. Well, you can see the quandary of names, quality, and marketing all at once.

Carlos Barberán's twenty-year prediction might have come dangerously true, but rather than depress one reader, it inspired him. And so Brent Black, an American close to forty when this book was first published, took a flyer on the Panama hat industry. His goal: encourage the weavers of the Montecristi region and restrict the Cuenca exporters from using—actually misusing—the name Montecristi. His motive: preserve the fine art of hat weaving and reward its weavers. It has only taken him more than thirty years, but Black has made a twenty-first century dent in the nineteenth-century hat trade.

To achieve his goal, Black established a school for weavers in the town of Pile (PEE-lay) in the Canton of Montecristi, where, historically, the best weavers are said to live. Pile children, at age fifteen, can earn an artisan certificate. After five years of training, they might rise to the level of Master Weaver—someone who can produce some 900 weaves per square inch. These are hats which can take up to six months apiece to weave, marketed as *finos*, or often, *superfinos*. A rare few weavers can reach the next level of Superior weaver—1,600 weaves per square inch, or forty rows to the inch, and only one weaver has, on commission, woven a silky 2,500 weaves per square inch. Black commissions these hats and, unlike most arrangements, pays weavers in advance, then more when the hat sells. Through this system weavers make considerably more than they would otherwise earn. About sixty students have graduated from this school and are now turning out high-quality hats. It's a singular approach for an industry that for generations has worked on the hat-by-hat sales method. And it avoids the exploitative excess the Panama hat business has often been accused of. If Ecuador had roadside adopt-a-highway signs, one would surely list Brent Black as the sponsor of the road leading into Pile.

Hats woven in the Canton of Montecristi using straw from the region have acquired an official Denomination of Origin (D.O.) of "Montecristi Hats" from the Instituto Ecuatoriano de la Propieded Intelectual. This legal status was established to prevent hats from elsewhere using the name of Montecristi to indicate quality and imply origin. "Once you create a mystique of an item's history, the value of that item increases," the intellectual property rights lawyer handling the Montecristi D.O. told me. "History and mystique are important to trademark." The hats are part of Ecuador's national patrimony. In the year 2000, the hat industry benefited by stabilization when the country converted its currency from the *sucre* to the dollar.

Panama hat creation, whether in the Montecristi region or hats woven in the Cuenca area, has one characteristic: the hats are woven by hand and hand only, with no mechanical devices involved. Accept no substitutes.

—*T.M.*

THE PANAMA HAT TRAIL

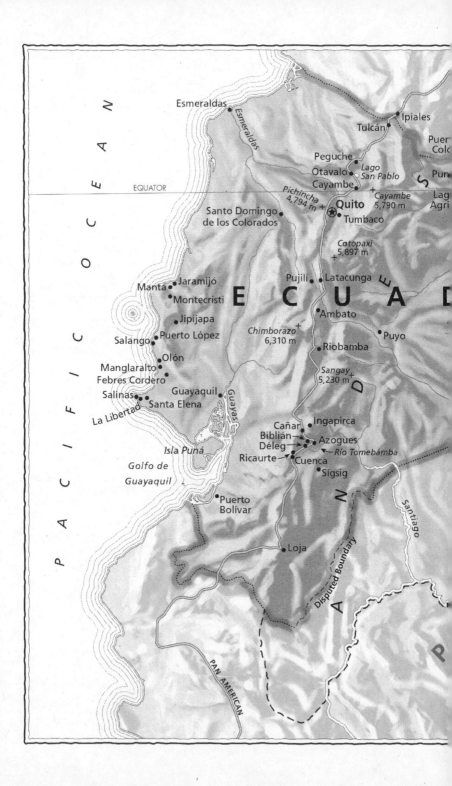

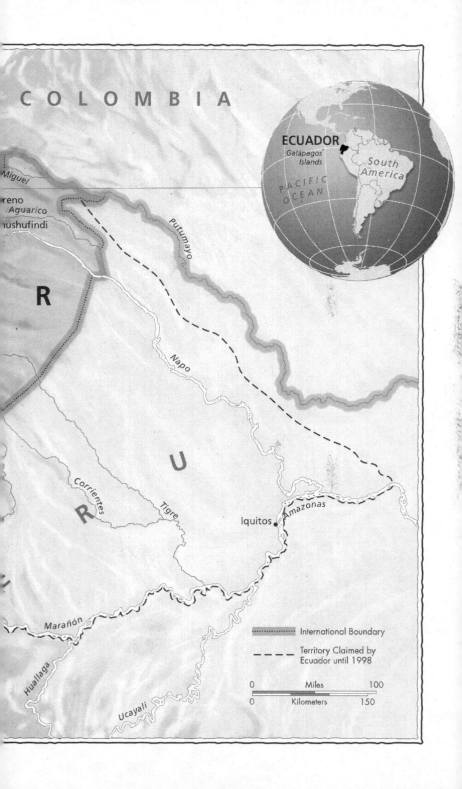

COLOMBIA

Miguel

reno
Aguarico

hushufindi

R

ECUADOR
Galápagos
Islands
PACIFIC
OCEAN
South
America

Putumayo

Napo

U

Corrientes

R

Tigre

Iquitos • Amazonas

Marañón

Huallaga

Ucayali

International Boundary

Territory Claimed by
Ecuador until 1998

0   Miles   100
0   Kilometers   150

INTRODUCTION

Where do Panama hats come from? One might sooner ask who was buried in Grant's tomb, except that the answer is not so obvious. Panama hats are made in Ecuador.

The major trading post for South American goods in the nineteenth and early twentieth centuries was at the Isthmus of Panama, the quickest and safest seafaring route to Europe and North America. Sugar, fruit, minerals, cloth, and dozens of other products passed through the isthmus on their way to market, Ecuadoran straw hats included. In the mid-1800s gold seekers from the East Coast rushing to California picked up the straw hats on their way west, and—for those who returned home—on their way back as well. A famous woodcut from 1850 shows seven scraggly gold-rushers just returned to the East from California via Panama sitting outside the Philadelphia Mint. Each is clutching bags bulging with gold dust, and each is wearing a Panama hat. Fifty years later, workers on the Panama Canal found the locally sold hats ideal for laboring in the tropical sun and, like the Forty-Niners, named them for their point of purchase rather than their place of origin. The name stuck.

To visit Ecuador under the best of conditions seemed unlikely. But to travel throughout the small country with only the vague notion of tracking down the straw-hat trade seemed absurd. The country, a fraction larger than the state of Colorado, is of marginal interest to all but the few Americans who can place it on a map and whose livelihood depends on its well-being. "You're going to Ecuador?" bewildered friends asked, invariably inquiring about the dangers of traveling in a country undergoing civil war. Like most people, they confused Ecuador with the other Latin country beginning with *E* and ending with *ador*.

In fact, Ecuador is relatively peaceful, lacking the intensity of guerrilla activity to which its better-known neighbors, Peru and Colombia, are prone. Its attitude toward the rest of South America is sufficiently enlightened that it could host a hemisphere-wide conference on human rights and have its participants welcomed by the nation's vice-president. Ecuadorans are basically squeamish when it comes to changes in government, and prefer their coups bloodless. After the hoopla of a new regime settles down, the only perceptible change to most of the country's nine million people is new letterhead on government stationery. Panama hat production has outlived theocratic rule, benevolent dictatorships, military juntas, and wobbly democracies. Ecuador's current experiment in democracy, which began in 1979, depends upon international crude-oil prices for its survival. Petroleum pumped from beneath the Amazon basin and from offshore deposits supports the national economy. In the not-too-distant past the country was a genuine banana republic, dependent upon that fruit and cacao as its major exports.

"Ecuador has a severe inferiority complex," a State Department officer told me before I left for South America. It was a comment easily dismissed as Foggy Bottom chauvinism, yet in meeting the people and traveling their land I found, surprisingly, many Ecuadorans echoing that sentiment. Ecuador is the butt of nationalistic jokes by Colombians to the north. It has been emasculated along its southeastern frontier by Peru. During World Cup soccer matches Ecuadorans are glued to their radios and cheer every goal, yet their own team invariably fails to qualify for international competition. Torrential rains cause utter crop failure and flood entire villages, devastating an already stagnant economy, yet the problem is solved not by bank loans or farm credits but by an international telethon with viewers in Ecuador and the United States donating money to save the country from destitution. And although *huasipungaje*, indentured servitude, officially ended in 1964, social progress in Ecuador seems to move only slightly faster than the giant tortoises on its famed Galápagos Islands. It is a low-profile country whose international obscurity is interrupted only for plane crashes, earthquakes, when its border war with Peru flares, or when one of its magnificent volcanoes erupts.

When a United States observer reported his impressions of Ecuador back to the president, he regretted that his "analysis is not entirely favorable . . . but the generous and friendly thing is to frankly depict the faults as well as the virtues of the country." The president in this case was not Donald J. Trump but Chester A. Arthur, during whose administration the United States began to flex its hemispheric muscle. "At present," the 1883 report concluded, "the elements on which to build a thriving nation are so buried in discord that they are difficult to discover."

Now, more than a century later, the discord is so buried that it seldom surfaces in a substantive way. Through this country, then, I traveled, initially for a few months, and then off and on over a period of three years. I went by foot, canoe, burro, and bus, taxi, train, plane, and steamship. Along the way I encountered evidence of the Inca Empire and United States foreign policy. My goal was to trace the origins of the Panama hat and follow its route from the basement of the Third World to the penthouse of the First. Yet the Panama hat trail, as I hoped it might, occasioned unanticipated twists and turns and afforded unexpected pleasures. The journey, then, became the search for the hat, and the hat the pretext for my journey.

A word about money: Repeat visits to South America allowed me to retrace my original journey several times. When I first arrived in Ecuador, its currency, the *sucre*, was 30 to the dollar, or 3.3 cents each. By the week I last departed, more than three years later, it had plummeted to 120 to the dollar, or just over .8 of a penny each. For the dollar-based traveler, Ecuador seemed to be having a half-price sale. Because the value of the *sucre* never held from one month to the next, attaching a *sucre* cost each time a price is mentioned in the book would create confusion and distort its relative worth. For consistency, I have given a dollar value to most prices, using the *sucre* when it is more illustrative. To best appreciate the fragility of the country's economy, understand that the largest denomination in Ecuador's currency is the 1,000-*sucre* note, today worth less than ten dollars. In 2000, Ecuador adopted the U.S. dollar as its domestic currency.

PART ONE

CHAPTER ONE

AN OPENING INTO HEAVEN

One night during my first week in South America some new friends took me to a rocky crest high up on the east side of Quito, the capital of Ecuador. To our east rose the fullest of moons, so frighteningly near and brilliant that we could almost have reached it with a stepladder. Below us glittered the city of 900,000 stretched out over the base of Pichincha, the 15,400-foot mountain that dominates the city from the west. Many miles away the snow-covered peaks along the "Avenue of Volcanoes," as the German naturalist Alexander von Humboldt called it, appeared gin clear. My friends swept their hands along an east-west arc to the north, indicating the approximate path of 0 degrees latitude, the Equator. At a slight angle to the Equator they pointed out the eastward route followed by sixteenth-century conquistador Francisco de Orellana, who led the first recorded expedition from the Andes down into the Amazon jungle and out to the Atlantic Ocean.

Turning south my hosts showed me where the pipeline carrying oil from the eastern jungle crosses the mountains on its way to the Pacific Coast. Gazing at the sky, they pointed out how the planets, the moon, and the stars arrange themselves above the Equator in a pattern far different from what we see in northern skies. The constellation Scorpio dominated overhead; the North Star rested just above the horizon. From our mountainside vantage point, the proud boast made of their city by Quiteños—the residents of Quito—becomes clear, that Quito is *un hueco en el cielo*, an opening into heaven.

My introduction to South America made an enormous impression. On our way up the mountainside we had passed through Bella Vista, a crowded and noisy neighborhood inhabited by poor *mestizos*—mixed blood—and Indians who always seemed to be carrying something on their backs. In the early evening small crowds formed around street-corner stands. Makeshift fires kept the food and people warm. Most men, women, and children wore hats. Some were Panamas, others felt, still others fabric. I asked a street vendor if I might touch his Panama. It was firm, almost hard, with a shellaclike stiffness. And they are not Panama hats, I was firmly but politely told. That is a misnomer. Here they are *sombreros de paja*—straw—and they come from Cuenca, a city to the south.

I wanted to linger in Quito before pushing on to Cuenca. I had read about Quito in travel journals dating back to its founding in 1534, and of the Inca settlement that predated Gonzalo Pizarro's arrival. It was a religious city, I knew, conservative of dress and custom, with churches practically every two blocks. Until the oil boom busted the north end of town wide open in the early 1970s, Quito's cultural and commercial life centered in a part of the city known for its narrow streets, colonial architecture, cramped quarters, and formal manners. *Un hueco en el cielo*, I repeated to anyone who would listen. What does this mean to you—is it really so? They believed it, everyone, fiercely proud of their ancient city and the overpowering volcanoes that dwarf it. "What does *un hueco en el cielo* mean to you?" an Indian from Ambato asked me. Well, I replied, that here you are so close to God, physically and spiritually, you can virtually peek into heaven. She smiled. "That's what most North Americans and Europeans say. To the Indians it means that God can look down upon us."

At 9,300 feet, Quito's air is so rarefied that the sun's rays beat down with deceptive strength. A brisk midday walk in the equatorial Andes leaves you sweating profusely. Near dusk, *garúa*—intense fog—rolls through the city, limiting vision to an arm's length. "The man who doesn't like clouds has no business coming to Ecuador," wrote the Belgian Henri Michaux in 1928. "They're the faithful dogs of the mountains." Clouds go through gymnastics at this altitude, first low hugging the ground, then high embracing Mount Cayambe or Pichincha, then settling briefly in the Chillos or Tumbaco valleys before finally returning again to ground level.

"It has been said of Quito," wrote Ludwig Bemelmans in his classic 1941 travel book *The Donkey Inside*, "that it has one hundred churches and one bathroom." The ratio has narrowed somewhat since his time, but the opulence and ornate glitter of the city's churches still overwhelm the adjoining plazas and the impoverished natives who walk upon them. To move among Quiteños in San Francisco Square is to sense the stability the Old City's plazas exert and to appreciate their dominance. The San Francisco church houses a series of convents, each of which appears larger than many conventional churches. The San Augustín church includes the room where, in 1809, Ecuador's Act of Independence was signed.

A visitor could wander through churches for days here—the danger of becoming "churched out" is always present—but the most imposing structures share the same characteristics: skillfully crafted religious scenes detailed along the walls, gold leaf covering the more important facades, and huge paintings, solemn and lifeless, from the Quiteño school, a style of art that flourished under Spanish rule. Outside most churches a constant but low-key hubbub reigns: Parishioners beg for money, offering in return candles, religious ornaments, or blessings. The churches Ecuadorans point to most with pride were constructed with forced Indian labor.

In 1978 the old part of town, so well preserved from its colonial days, was added to UNESCO's World Heritage list of sites deemed to be "of outstanding universal value," an honor that carries only one stipulation—to preserve and protect its integrity. Thrilled with its newly won international status, the Quito city government immediately violated the stipulation and constructed a brand-new municipal building in the middle of the Old City.

The new section of town appears more European than Latin. It is centered around Amazonas Avenue, a spiffy shopping district filled with fine restaurants, classy hotels, quality bookstores, high-rise glass-walled office buildings, and shoeshine boys. La Mariscal, as it is called, resembles Mexico City's Zona Rosa in many ways, catering to the top of a bottom-heavy city. I made a habit of taking morning coffee there at the Pastelería París, a sidewalk café run by an Italian named Alfonso and his wife, Isabela. Often Alfonso would show up on his black motorcycle while his wife walked in with their large and woolly sheepdog. The coffee was invariably terrible, but the morning paper was always ready and Alfonso usually had a cheerful word about the latest scandal or crisis. One morning I found the place closed without explanation. "He's probably out of town," another regular said.

"He'll be back tomorrow." The next day Alfonso appeared—not on the street, however, but in the papers. He had been involved in some check-passing racket worth hundreds of thousands of dollars. Police picked him up trying to slip across the border into Colombia wearing a disguise. "His long-haired blond wig made him look ridiculous," the newspaper said.

Parking on the side streets in La Mariscal can be tricky. Police in white gloves keep traffic moving on Amazonas, their slow, fluid arm motion signaling a light change from green to red. Each block usually has a human parking meter in a doorman's uniform. He watches over the parking spaces, jealously guarding his turf for his regulars. When he spots a customer coming, he walks to the middle of the street like a traffic cop and stops cars so that his regular can ease into the curbside space. He watches over the car while its driver is away and expects in return a tip of thirty cents or so. One human parking meter, whose domain includes a number of Mercedes, comes to work prepared for early morning and evening chill with a scarf wrapped tightly around his face at the mouth, as if its purpose is to prevent him from speaking. He hopes some day to pass his job on to his son, he said, so that he too could oversee the parking of Mercedes Benzes.

One day the city of Quito bought some surplus double-decker buses from London. Instead of slovenly drivers, crowded aisles, broken windows, incessant honking, jostling at the door, impromptu stops, and screeching brakes, these snazzy blue double-deckers had fixed stops, drivers in ties, comfortable seats, clean floors, and sliding windows. To ride them required a ticket, usually available at a kiosk near each stop, costing a couple of *sucres* more than the fare for regular buses. The imported buses traveled from Carolina Park at one end of Amazonas Avenue, to the airport at the other. The novelty and efficiency of such civilization—European yet!—rolling through town made the double-deckers a success. One morning, a double-decker drove by as I sipped my morning coffee (same lousy coffee, different café) and read in the newspaper some instructions for Quiteños on the proper way to board a bus. "At some bus stops," said *El Comercio*, "users of public transportation have the good habit of forming lines for boarding buses or *colectivos*. Lamentably, at other stops the public crowds the bus, impeding the passage of children, women, and the elderly. This picture should be imitated by all citizens." Above was a photo showing forty people politely lined up single-file at a bus stop. The headline read: AN EXAMPLE TO FOLLOW.

A monument to Francisco de Orellana sits near the Hotel Quito overlooking the valley on the road to Guápulo, a semi-rural hillside neighborhood. The center of Guápulo is its Sanctuary, a popular spot to take in a Sunday morning mass. After a five-minute walk down a dirt road from the church, the houses get increasingly sparse. Some appear to have had no occupants for years. At one abandoned and utterly dilapidated adobe house I found an Indian woman sitting on the cement foundation. She was waiting for the return of the owner, her *patrón* for many years. Did I know where he was or have any word of him? He had left more than a decade earlier.

The Hotel Quito lies in a part of town called Gringo Gulch. Expensive homes and apartment towers line the streets, providing a habitat for embassy staff from the United States and elsewhere. Most have locked gates; some have armed guards. Workers for Texaco and its subcontractors live here as well.

At one end of Gringo Gulch rests a monument to Winston Churchill; at the other, one to Abraham Lincoln. The Churchill statue was a gift to the City of Quito from Great Britain; the one of Lincoln, a gift from the United States community of Quito. During Great Britain's little war with Argentina over the Falkland Islands in 1982, Sir Winston got a regular paint job—each week a bucket of a different bright color was dumped on his head and dripped down his clothes. Every now and then a new slogan appears on Lincoln's monument—GRINGOS GET OUT! was the last one I saw—but usually it stays unmolested. Anti-Soviet graffiti is not uncommon. RUSSIA—MURDERER OF PRIESTS was a recent one, a few streets down from GORBACHEV—OUT OF AFGHANISTAN.

Gringo in Ecuador means not just someone from the United States but from Europe as well. It is a generic word and, unlike many other Latin American countries, here it is more often neutral and benign than contemptuous and challenging. In Ecuador *norteamericanos* experience little of the overt animosity we have earned elsewhere.

The official residence of the United States ambassador adjoins the Hotel Quito on an estate equipped with a pool, a clay tennis court, and

Marine guards. The British Embassy faces the Quito, and next to it, El Pub—Bar Inglés. The Pub caters to British and United States expatriates who eat fish and chips, swap stories of Ecuadoran inefficiency, and tell tales of hunting for gold in the jungle. "The oil field trash stays out," says Pub co-owner Machete, his nickname earned during his years as a South American salesman for the company that manufactures machetes. "They know they're not wanted." Conversation glides from W. Somerset Maugham and Graham Greene to poorly laid fantasies to resurrect the Inca Atahualpa, stage a coup, capture the shrimp export market, or lead the Auca and Jívaro Indians in revolution.

An illegal alien from Scotland explained her plight to the goalie on The Pub's soccer team. "My situation is impossible here," she said. "I can't stay, and I can't leave the country either. Do you suppose this means I'll forever remain in Ecuador? I'm the wrong color! But I'm beginning to think I'm Ecuadoran. Maybe one of my students can help me. I teach English to Ecuadoran police. They're *so* slow. Why, I had better luck teaching English to Vietnamese refugees in Canada! Reading Lewis Carroll is really the only way to make sense of this place. I'm thinking of writing *Through the Andean Looking Glass.*" She quoted from *The Snark* and *Alice*: "'What I tell you three times is true.' 'Jam to-morrow and jam yesterday—but never jam *to-day.*' Living in Quito is like that."

International traveling salesmen selling heavy machinery to Texaco or the government relax at The Pub and chat about the Miami airport, what government official in which country needs his palm greased, and where to find a good meal in La Paz, Bolivia. White-collar dreamers, expatriates down on their luck, and failed mercenaries drift through with regularity. It's a great place to practice your English, especially if English is the only language you know.

I packed for Cuenca on a Sunday to look at the Panama hat trade, preparing to take the forty-minute, thirteen-dollar flight the next morning. "I wouldn't do that," a Quito businesswoman advised. "Monday's when all the accidents happen on the Quito-to-Cuenca run. It may be superstitious, but I never fly to Cuenca on a Monday." She handed me a copy of *Vuelo Sin Retorno* (*Flight without Return*), a best seller in Ecuador about the plane crash that killed Jaime Roldós. Roldós had been the first president elected after a military junta yielded to civilian rule for another stab at democracy in 1979. He was flying not to Cuenca but farther south to Loja when his plane went way off course and crashed into a mountainside. Since then a number of other flights south through the Andes, usually to Cuenca, have also lost their bearings and crashed. *Vuelo Sin Retorno* prompted a healthy round of conspiracy theories about whom to blame for the president's death—the Peruvians (another battle in their intermittent border war), the missionaries (Roldós had just evicted the Summer Institute of Linguistics, the country's leading North American Bible-thumpers), Cuban-backed guerrillas (Jack Anderson's theory), or the CIA. The CIA theory gained instant credibility, first on general principle, and second because a large part of *Inside the Company: CIA Diary*, Philip Agee's account of his years with the CIA, devotes itself to his clandestine activities in Ecuador.

Roldós became an instant martyr. Posters of him went up throughout the country, and, as the suddenly deceased youthful president in a newly formed democracy, he was afforded John Kennedy status. The government investigated the crash with outside help and convincingly ruled out sabotage. This was disappointing to those of us who love a good conspiracy, but by then we had run out of theories anyway.

CHAPTER TWO

CUENCA BY NIGHT

"Of all the earth, as far as I know it, Cuenca has the most perfect climate," wrote Harry A. Franck, whose meanderings through South America in the early twentieth century led to the book *Vagabonding Down the Andes.* "Always cool enough to be mildly invigorating to mind and body, yet never cold, it is unexcelled as a place for dreamy loafing."

These last five words heightened my anticipation months before I first arrived. Franck stayed in Cuenca long enough to learn its charms and frustrations, both extremes still in abundance. I took his advice to get some business cards made up before leaving for South America. "The man who has his name printed on bits of cardboard, to exchange with regal courtesy and profound bows with every upper-class acquaintance, is instantly accepted," he wrote. "Indeed, visiting cards should be as fixed a part of every Andean traveler's equipment as heavy boots." One cannot even accidentally bump into a stranger on a bus without the ritual exchange of cards, I quickly found. Mine included my name, home address, and the word *escritor,* writer. Although it showed no business or institutional affiliation, it gave me immediate credibility with all classes, for in a land where literacy is still a distant goal, foreign writers are welcomed as highly respected oddities.

This notoriety garnered me an invitation to give a talk before a class at the Universidad Estatal de Cuenca my second day in town. The course, an advanced-level seminar, was called Culture and Civilization of the English-Speaking Countries and met in the late afternoon. It was taught by an expatriate from the States who had been in the country for more than a decade. He was one of twenty-five United States citizens living in Cuenca, a city of 130,000. "This semester they've been studying Jefferson and Hamilton. They know they are at the start of their own democracy, and they study U.S. history intently. Although their country goes back centuries, they sense they are at a new beginning."

A dozen students sat at small desks in a small classroom. While I was being introduced, scores of students, then hundreds, hurried by the room. The teacher stuck his head outside. "Well, class is over for the day," he announced. "They got a *permiso*." Everyone stood up and filed out.

"What happened? I don't understand."

"Sometimes I don't either, but I just accept it. What happened is that a student group got a permit from the administration to call off classes and hold a rally in the main auditorium. They can do it prac- tically anytime they want. It wreaks havoc on my lesson plans. These things take place almost every week."

I went outside and joined the throng. As I walked into the audi- torium a student leader was inveighing against the government for a recent rise in the cost of living while poor people starved. "Everything costs more now—bread, sugar, gasoline. The government wants it this way. So do imperialists and the rich. It's in their interest!" His speech was punctuated by shouts of approval, applause, and wolf whistles at the women on the platform. "Considering the misery and exploitation that the working class lives in, devaluation has raised the cost of living too high. The government has brought the country to virtual bank- ruptcy and total indebtedness." The national currency was in the mid- dle of an alarming slide, losing two-thirds of its value within about a year. "And the Malvinas Islands belong to Argentina," he put in as an afterthought, integrating South America's burning issue of the day into his speech. "The United States is to blame!"

Evidently I was the enemy in their midst, and I glanced around ner- vously. Friendly faces from the Culture and Civilization class grinned back. "Students have demonstrated in Quito," the speaker went on. "Students in Guayaquil have also marched through the streets." He paused for dramatic effect. "We should do the same!" Thunderous applause greeted his suggestion, followed by rounds of chanting.

The group left the auditorium and slowly marched through the streets, yelling slogans in rhythmic cadence and blocking traffic. I moved along its outer fringe. We were for the poor, against the rich;

for "the people," against imperialism; for justice, against the United States. We wanted lower prices on basic necessities, and accused the government of promoting starvation. A splinter group broke away as we crossed over a bridge spanning the Tomebamba River. They burned tires in the middle of the street; then they burned a U.S. flag and ran it over with a four-wheel-drive Chevy Trooper. Dusk approached as the main body, thinning but still vocal, joined up with a group of workers and *campesinos* just finishing up its own protest rally at Calderón Park in the heart of town. "Considering the miserable exploitation that exists in the Ecuadoran working class," the workers' leader shouted, "the cost of living has reached its limit!"

Cheers for his speech were suddenly drowned out by the twenty-member municipal marching band, consisting of clarinet, trumpets, cymbals, saxophone, and tuba—playing, what?—the music was indecipherable, but the spirit and volume were high. The grand *fiesta* honoring St. Peter and St. Paul was underway, a week-long celebration centering in the park. Fifty little girls in pint-sized wedding gowns emerged from the cathedral, their first communion over. Evening came to the plaza as the little girls, nuns, and demonstrators mingled with townspeople who gravitated family by family to the square. The last of the demonstrators bolted from the crowd to set several automobile tires afire, but, except for the odor, their revelry blended in with the festivities.

Cuenca is among the most Roman Catholic cities in Latin America—conservative, religious, and correct. Even the pope would be considered a backslider here, but he would appreciate Cuenca's municipal motto: *Primero Dios, Después Vos.* First God, Then You. I heard about a Cuencano who sent his daughter to college in the United States. A few months later a business associate was to visit the States, and the father asked his friend to check up on his daughter. Upon his return the businessman lunched with the father. "I've got terrible news for you," the businessman said in a somber tone. "Your daughter has become a pro—" The rumble of a passing truck drowned his words.

"Oh, that's awful," said his unhappy companion. "I raised her so properly, took her to Mass every Sunday, sent her to the right schools—why I even had the bishop himself officiate at her communion. Where did I go wrong?"

"Yes, such a pity," consoled the businessman. "I was shocked to learn that she had become a prostitute."

"Oh!" said the father, much relieved. "I thought you said she'd become a Protestant!"

Two cathedrals stare into the plaza. To the west is the New Cathedral, built in 1880. Across the plaza the Metropolitan Cathedral, built three centuries earlier, faces it. For the *fiesta* honoring St. Peter and St. Paul, a thousand people crowded in between the two cathedrals, drinking and gambling, drinking and shooting off fireworks, drinking and eating, drinking and singing.

Small card tables with Coleman stoves on top were set up throughout the plaza. A pot filled with water and cinnamon bark rested on each stove. Bottles of Cristal—clear sugarcane liquor—were lined up next to the stoves. For ten cents the middle-aged Indian vendor would pour a little Cristal into a shot glass and fill the rest with a ladleful from her simmering caldron. The glass had just come back from the dishwasher—her six-year-old barefoot son, beneath the table, who dipped each glass into a vat of lukewarm water and smeared it dry with a rag. The recipe for *canelazo*: two parts cinnamon-water to one part Cristal. Add a squeeze of lemon, if you please. A warm glow results.

Gambling took place at other tables. Roulette and other games using crudely built spinning wheels, craps with hand-carved dice, fast-moving pebbles under thimbles, and still more primitive devices lured petty gamblers who bought into them for two cents each. Fast-talking pitchmen, Indians all, ran most games like barkers on a carnival midway. Their faces were illuminated by the soft glow of the nearby Coleman stoves. Their children slept soundly through the noise on the ground beneath their tables. Fireworks were launched into the sky from bamboo structures thirty feet high, each the project of a neighborhood for this one night's use. Paper globes rose into the night sky like hot-air balloons. A blind man in sunglasses sat on the ground singing Andean wedding songs into a jerry-built loudspeaker. His wife circled the small crowd that gathered, selling a book of the marriage songs for forty cents a copy. Most people wore Panama hats, the hat for peasants and *campesinos*, both men and women. Debonair in the Northern Hemisphere, the Panama hat identifies you as one of the lower-class majority in the Southern. No self-respecting member of

Cuenca's aristocracy would ever be seen wearing a locally made hat of native straw.

Tooth-rotting confections sent a thick aroma through the carnival air. Potatoes and freshly popped corn added to the smell, mixed with meat, candy apples, rice, sugar cane, *canelazo*, and what still hung in the air from the burning tires. *Mestizo* and upper-class kids flirted on park benches, posing for photographers whose aging cameras balanced on wooden tripods. Pickup trucks slowly circled the plaza, with children in the back smooching, laughing, yelling, and waving to the happy celebrants.

As the *fiesta* died down and the firecrackers slowed to one every couple of minutes, two Indians walked over to the Hotel El Dorado, peeked into the bar, and blew their last *sucres* of the night on the casino's roulette wheel. They played red five and walked away before the silver ball plunked down in black sixteen. A truncated beggar with gnarled hands leaned against the hotel window. A legless boy rode home on a hand-pedaled bicycle.

CHAPTER THREE

WITH THE EXPORTERS

Cuenca's Panama hat exporters are the fulcrum on the scale between the weavers and the marketplace. A business directory provided a starting point, and I visited a handful to learn about their trade. Moisés Bernal Bravo met me at his Panama hat factory the morning after the *fiesta*. Bernal lives and works next to a city park on the east side of town. A hundred of his Panamas were spread out drying in the park. Neighbors walked around them; none were stolen. "Most of the hats are woven in small towns nearby, not in Cuenca itself," Bernal told me. "They use a straw called *toquilla*. You know, of course, that 'Panama hat' is a misnomer. None are made there.

"The weavers bring their hats to the special *toquilla* straw market in Cuenca on Thursday, in Azogues on Saturday, and in Biblián on Sunday. That's where they sell their woven hats and buy the straw for the next week. There are smaller markets in other towns too. The hats are sold to *comisionistas*," to middlemen.

"Let me show you something." He took me into his *bodega*—a storage room—filled with dozens of ceiling-high stacks of Panamas. "You see these?" He tapped a pile of light-brown hats designed with rows of air holes in the crown. "They go to Brazil. These over here"— he motioned toward another stack with wider brims—"they are for Mexico. And those"—smiling, he pointed to piles of hats near the door—"those go to your country." In an adjoining room two young men inspected hundreds of hats one by one. "They're looking for imperfections. That's our quality control department. My children work for me too. The eldest handles the business end of things. His wife speaks some English."

Bernal called for coffee from his secretary. I asked if the weavers who make the hats from the *toquilla* straw had any idea what the hats cost in the States, or even where they go once they're sold to the middlemen. "Ah, the weavers are ignorant and illiterate. They know they're exploited, but they're exploited in everything they do. They sell hats to the *comisionistas*, but they don't know or care what happens to the hats next. It doesn't affect them. They wear the cheapest straw hats themselves.

"In Biblián, the best weavers weave by the light of the moon. In general, the finest hats are woven when it's cloudy and slightly overcast. Here, have some coffee." His secretary spooned some instant coffee into a cup and added hot water. I pretended to like it and Bernal continued. "Although I've been in this business for many years, I still don't understand your country. The U.S. is spoiled. They want the absolute best hats. They are obsessed! If there's the slightest imperfection in the color, then they won't take the hat, even if the weave is the most intricate and the style the most fashionable.

"We sold ten thousand hats a week to the States during World War Two. It's still a tremendous market, even though sales to North America have shrunk recently." He sipped his coffee and handed me a nicely styled Panama, Mexican brown. "Here, won't you accept this as a gift from Ecuador?"

I thanked him and asked, "What do you do with the imperfect hats the U.S. won't take?"

"That's easy. I ship them to Brazil."

Across town, Homero Ortega was equally eager to show me his export operation. He had just returned from the weekly straw fair a few blocks from his business, and middlemen were drifting in and out with piles of hats they'd bought at the market. Stacks of Panamas were everywhere. You couldn't walk a straight line for more than ten feet without bumping into one. Iron hat presses from the United States, most at least fifty years old, stood off to the side, ready to give shape to the soft hat bodies.

"This company is a hundred years old," the patriarch of the Ortega hat company said. "My father Aurelio started it. I joined him when I was sixteen. That was fifty years ago. My children will take it over from me. As recently as the late seventies we sold sixty thousand hats a month to Brazil alone. Now, with their economic problems, they buy only a hundred thousand a year. I think we export more hats than anyone else in town." And again: "You know, by the way, that we don't call them 'Panama hats.' That's a mistaken name we have to live with."

Ortega's export operation is run out of an old colonial building. Like so many homes in Cuenca, from the outside all you can see is a drab wall and a wooden door promising little behind it. Inside, however, is a sizable two-story house with a large courtyard in the middle, illuminated by a skylight. Hats dried in its middle. Floors of tile, marble, and cement had loose strands of *toquilla* straw all over in a sort of orderly mess. A showroom greeted customers, displaying a wide selection of Panamas. The few organized tours that pass through town often stop at Ortega's place to buy hats direct from the factory.

"My son Bosco here spent fifteen years in the United States," said Ortega, introducing us. "He's the *subgerente* here," the assistant manager. Bosco had lived in Connecticut working at a number of restaurants, the names of which he reeled off with minimal prompting. "Once Paul Newman came in to one of them!"

Bosco took me to his house for lunch. While I sipped a drink with him and his wife in their living room, the cook finished preparing our meal. "Sometimes we get hats that can't be used by themselves," Señora Ortega said. "With those, we simply weld two imperfect hats together as one. You can't tell the difference. Bosco's father was the innovator of that process."

Back at the factory Homero Ortega elaborated on the rest of the process. "When the hats come in from the weavers, the outer brim is incomplete, so each hat has hundreds of loose strands of *paja toquilla* hanging from the edge. We buy them this way. We employ our own hat finishers to complete the outermost part, tie the loose ends together, and snip off the excess. Look." He handed me a hat bought just an hour earlier at the market. A thick fringe of loose straw, each strand at least six inches long, hung from the brim. "Our finishers complete the hats at their homes. We paid sixty cents for this hat here at the market. The finisher makes another few cents for each hat he works on. We don't exploit the workers. We pay vacation time and give them all the benefits."

Bosco motioned me out into the hall and offered me some coffee. I took a sip and feigned pleasure. "My father and I would like you to have this hat, special from the Ortega family." He handed me a Panama from a pile destined for Brazil, then started placing stickers inside some hats going to Mexico. The stickers said HECHO EN MEXICO— Made in Mexico. He noticed I was watching. "They want it this way. It's better for their business."

Señora Paredes greeted me at her husband's exporting company. The Paredes family lived above their hat plant, although with all the piles of hats on the carpeting, on furniture, and on the television, it was hard to tell where the shop ended and the home began. I declined a cup of coffee. "Here is where we clean and bleach the hats," her son Jorge said, leading me into a smaller room. "We use sodium sulfite and also peroxide. After that the hats go into the presses, and then we soften them again." A worker was pounding the hat brims with a mallet, a softening process every hat undergoes. "You can't hit them too hard or the straw will break," the pounder said. "But if you tap too lightly it has no effect at all."

He continued pounding while Jorge sat me down in his office. He pulled a sheet of onionskin stationery out of a drawer and put it in his typewriter:

> Information about possible trade in *sombreros de paja toquilla*. Standard price for finished hats: U.S. $46 a dozen. Standard price for hat bodies: U.S. $42 a dozen. FOB Cuenca, Ecuador. Conditions of payment: An open letter of credit from a U.S. bank. Quantities: Whatever quantity you want can be shipped within ninety days. In stock: At the moment we have 2,400 hat bodies ready for shipping.
> Sincerely, _____

He signed it with a signature resembling that of every Latin American businessman: a series of neatly scripted compressed parallel curved lines, carried out with a flourish and utterly illegible. "I'd like to start selling hats to the United States," he said. "Right now ninety-five percent of my business is with Brazil. You know, they really shouldn't be called Panamas at all." He put his sales letter inside an envelope and the envelope inside a straw cowboy hat. "Here"—he patted the brim— "take this as a gift so you'll remember us."

Every exporter I went to had the same sort of operation. He'd buy untrimmed hats from middlemen who bought them from the weavers; then his workers would finish the trim and wash, bleach, clean, treat, shape, and soften the hats and prepare them for shipping. Technically, what they export are unblocked hat bodies, not completed hats. Everyone in the trade lamented the hat's international name. Ecuadoran consuls abroad were once instructed to attach stickers reading PANAMA HATS ARE MADE IN ECUADOR to all their correspondence. The gambit failed, reported Victor von Hagen in *Ecuador the Unknown*. The consul to San Francisco complained that people remarked: "I see they are now making Panama hats in Ecuador."

When each exporter presented me with a hat and a cup of coffee, I accepted the former and came to decline the latter. The few exceptions I invariable regretted. Is the coffee there measured by the cupful or by its viscosity? For a coffee-producing country, Ecuador offers surprisingly distasteful coffee—bitter and lacking richness. Most restaurants serve either instant coffee or *esencia*—coffee boiled down to its thickest form and placed on the table in a small bottle. Pour a little in your cup and fill the rest with boiling water. In Ecuador, Ludwig Bemelmans wrote, "If you love coffee, you must bring your own. They cook the coffee long enough in advance, brewing a foul ink of it which is kept in a bottle. Half a cupful of this dye is poured out, the sugar bowl emptied into it, and a little milk added on." I checked back through the travel literature to see if this were simply a modern prejudice. It isn't; virtually every written account of travel through South America over the past century notes displeasure with coffee in Ecuador. I was heartened to find that some homes and restaurants have taken to serving better coffee smuggled in from neighboring Colombia.

The next day I saw five more exporters. Enrique Malo was the oldest hat dealer in town. Eighty-four years old, he sat with his brother in an ascetic office on the second floor of their factory. They wore high starched collars and looked like characters in a Dickens story. In slow but flawless English learned during his years at Oxford, Enrique told me he had once served as governor of the province of Azuay, of which Cuenca was the capital.

The manager of Ernest J. French & Co. narrated a year-by-year history of the firm, founded by the secretary of the British Embassy in

1933. Next I saw Nicolás Jara, who told me that in 1914 his father used to pack hats on mules for the four-day trek to the port at Guayaquil. Finally I visited Mauro Santana, who announced that he had been to the United States twice. "I wear a Panama when I go to New York." He gave his impression of a New Yorker by glancing nervously back and forth between his watch and the top of some imagined skyscraper. "I love to listen to the British speak English. But the Americans?" He made a face. "They corrupt the language. They are *los monos de inglés*," the monkeys of English. He showed me a *superfino*—a hat woven tightly and finely with the thinnest and lightest of straw. "The only person who can wear this one," he proclaimed triumphantly, "is Queen Elizabeth."

Before visiting one last factory I stopped at Rancho Chileno for lunch. Ecuador has a history of welcoming, or at least tolerating, refugees from other countries. This includes refugees from Chile, some of whom arrived during Salvador Allende's socialist coalition government. Most have come since then to escape the dictatorship of Augusto Pinochet. Whenever they came, one result is that Ecuador boasts a fair number of good Chilean restaurants. Rancho Chileno, next to the airport, served terrific *empanadas*, a fried doughy outside sealed around flavorful steamy meat. Tropical drinks made from fruits unknown complement the food.

I ate my *empanadas* on the patio, where I bought a copy of *Vistazo*—a sort of Ecuadoran *People*—from an eight-year-old vendor named Hernando. When he wasn't kicking a soccer ball around with his brother in the adjoining lot, he hovered near the tables hawking magazines and keeping an eye out for departing diners. One tableful got up to pay and Hernando lunged upon their unfinished desserts, inhaling the gooey remains of a banana split into his near-toothless mouth. A man of twenty or so sat nearby watching. When the boy got near him, the man reached out, grabbed him, and cuffed him about the ears as he took the money the boy had made selling magazines. Hernando fought back his tears and returned to kicking the soccer ball with his brother.

That afternoon I visited my last hat exporter for the day. He confirmed Harry A. Franck's remark that aside from studying the professions, "He who does not deal in 'panama' hats has hardly an opening in

Cuenca." Gerardo Serrano first studied economics and business, then found himself dealing in Panama hats. His plant was on Pío Bravo, a cobblestone street so narrow that two cars passing each other would clink side-view mirrors. It is the oldest street in an old town. Serrano looks like a New York garment-district man, with a friendly round face above a rounding body. He wore a dark three-piece suit, customary for Cuenca businessmen, and over it a white smock. He had entered the hat business for himself in the early 1950s after serving as business adviser to one of the other companies. "I wasn't satisfied with the way they were weaving and finishing the hats here. So I visited the United States and Europe to see how they finish and trim their hats. I learned English and accounting from the LaSalle Extension School. The courses came by mail." He pointed to recent issues of a Harvard Business School publication. "I brought the industry into the twentieth century," he boasted in his eighteenth-century office. He showed off a trophy his hats had won in a competition in Buenos Aires. "And soon," he said, "I'll be moving into a brand-new factory my son is designing. He's an engineer.

"It's too bad you weren't here two weeks ago. There was an exhibition about the Panama hat trade at CIDAP" (*El Centro Interamericano de Artesanías y Artes Populares*—Inter-American Popular Arts and Crafts Center, a branch of the Organization of American States). "The display was put up by students from the state university. Here's the brochure." The pamphlet emphasized the role of the weaver in the hat trade. "The students have a tendency toward Marxism, communism, and populism. They are more interested in politics than in their studies. That's the way it is in underdeveloped countries. They say that the poor weaver makes so little and when the hat is sold at last it costs so much. They don't take into account all that we do to each hat before we sell it.

"During vacation time the children in the countryside weave hats. They learn from their mothers. It's supplementary income for each family while they watch the cattle, cook meals, and take care of the house and the baby. They start as early as six in the morning and weave in stretches of two or three hours until midday. Women are better at weaving *toquilla* hats because the straw is more supple and pliable and their hands can adjust to it better. Country people—they don't have clean hands. When we wash the hats we take out the grease. Then they get bleached and dyed, followed by ironing and pressing. Besides the United States, Mexico, and Brazil, I ship to Argentina, Uruguay, Paraguay, Germany, Italy, Switzerland, and England." He brightened up—"And I even sell a few to France!"

Serrano's business day was over, and he offered me a ride back to my hotel. The sun had ceased warming the air, and an early evening chill was coming on. As he left his ancient wooden plant, he secured the door with a ten-pound shackle joining two horseshoe hooks at the bottom. The man in the three-piece suit slowly folded himself over to ground level to latch his weighty colonial padlock. Silhouetted against the dark building on the ancient street at nightfall, Serrano's black suit blended seamlessly.

CHAPTER FOUR

THE BUS PLUNGE HIGHWAY

One of the hatters told me how to reach Victor González, an importer of raw *toquilla* straw from the coast. When I walked into his house, he started to hand me a fifty-*sucre* note. (The *sucre* was worth slightly more than a penny at the time.) I hadn't yet introduced myself. "No, no," I protested, "there must be some mistake. I telephoned this morning and spoke with your daughter, Fanny, about—" Fanny, entering the front courtyard, interrupted. "He thinks you're from the government," she apologized. "I'll tell him again what you're interested in." As she explained, her father relaxed somewhat, and he led the way to a room filled with large sacks tightly wrapped in light cloth, about three feet by five feet, holding the raw straw.

"These are called *bultos*. They come like this from the coast. If you're going up to the town they come from, take this, will you?" He wrote a note to his suppliers listing the prices he was paying for *bultos* that week. I was closing in on the beginning of the trail.

"You'll be going to Febres Cordero."

I stopped and stared. That was the name of the country's president, elected in 1984. "He's got nothing to do with it," Fanny said. "It was named for his grandfather, a military officer."

"From Guayaquil," her father continued, "take a bus to La Libertad, and from there to Febres Cordero. It's easy. Make sure you give them my price list."

To reach the town of Febres Cordero I took a bus to Guayaquil— at 1.6 million, the country's most populous city. The 150-mile ride started smoothly despite my apprehension. Bus rides through Latin America have always induced fear in me, brought on by years of reading one-paragraph bus-plunge stories used by newspapers in the States as fillers on the foreign-news page. The datelines change, but the headlines always include the words *bus plunge*, as in 12 DIE IN SRI LANKA BUS PLUNGE, OR CHILEAN BUS PLUNGE KILLS 31.

"We can count on one every couple of days or so," an editor at the *New York Times* once told me. "They're always ready when we need them." Never more than two sentences long, a standard bus-plunge piece will usually include the number feared dead, the identity of any group on board—a soccer team, church choir, or school bus—and the distance of the plunge from the capital city. The words *ravine* and *gorge* pop up often. Most of the stories come from Third World countries, the victims constituting just a fraction of the faceless brown-skinned masses. "A hundred Pakistanis going off a mountain in a bus make less of a story than three Englishmen drowning in the Thames," noted foreign correspondent Mort Rosenblum in *Coups & Earthquakes*. Is there a news service that does nothing but supply daily papers with bus-plunge stories? Peru and India seem to generate the most coverage; perhaps the wire services have more stringers in the Andes and Himalayas than anywhere else.

If an Ecuadoran bus driver survives a plunge fatal to others, according to Moritz Thomsen in *Living Poor*, "he immediately goes into hiding in some distant part of the country so that the bereaved can't even up the score. There are rumors of whole villages down in the far reaches of the Amazon basin populated almost entirely by bus drivers. This is probably apocryphal . . ."

If you anticipate a bus trip in Latin America, go through the following checklist prior to boarding:

☐ Look at the tires. If three or more of the six tires (most buses include two rear sets of two each) are totally bald, the probability of bus plunge increases. Visible threads on the tires means a blowout is imminent.

☐ Does the bus have at least one windshield wiper? Good. If it's on the driver's side, so much the better. Try to avoid buses whose windshields are so crowded with decals, statues, and pictures that the driver has only a postcard-size hole through which to see the future. Shrines to saints, pious homilies, boastful bumper stickers, and religious trinkets do not reflect the safety of a bus. Jesus Christ and Che Guevara are often worshiped on the same decal. This should give neither high hopes nor nagging suspicion.

☐ The driver's sobriety isn't a factor. The presence of his wife or girl-friend is. If she's along, she will usually sit immediately behind him, next to him, or on his lap. He will want to impress her with his daring at the wheel, but he will also go to great lengths not to injure her. If he has no girlfriend or wife, the chances of gorge dive increase.

☐ You can't check the bus for brakes. Once I asked a driver in Guatemala about the brakes on his bus. "Look," he said, "the bus is stopped, isn't it? Then the brakes must work."

☐ On intercity buses, seats are often assigned before boarding. Refuse the seat directly behind the driver or in the front right. If your ride takes place during the day, you'll be subjected to at least one heart-skip a minute as your bus casually passes a truck on an uphill blind curve or goes head-to-head with an oncom-ing bus. At night the constant glare of approaching headlights will shine in your eyes. At any hour, the driver's makeshift radio speaker will dangle closer to your ears than you'd like.

☐ Always have your passport ready. Random military inspections take place when you least expect them. I once delayed a bus full of cross-country travelers for ten minutes a couple of miles out-side Esmeraldas, on the Pacific Coast south of Colombia, while frantically searching first for my bag atop the bus, then my pass-port within the bag.

In defense of Latin-American buses: They go everywhere. *Everywhere.* No road is so dusty, bumpy, unpopulated, narrow, or obscure that a bus doesn't rumble down it at least once every twenty-four hours. The fare is very little—Cuenca to Guayaquil cost less than three dollars—and, barring plunges, they almost always reach their destination. If your window opens, you'll get a view of the countryside unmatched in painting or postcard. Your seatmate may be an aging *campesina* on her way home or a youthful Indian on his first trip to the big city. Dialects of Spanish and Quechua unknown to linguists float past you. Chickens, piglets, and children crowd the aisles or ride on top.

At Cuenca's *terminal terrestre*, the bus station, I had a choice of taking a regular bus or an *aerotaxi* to Guayaquil. The former travels slower, hence it is theoretically safer. The latter, a small twenty-four seater, whizzes along far faster, has less leg room, and tends to be more plunge-prone. I resisted the odds and took an *aerotaxi*.

The trip, five and a half hours long, begins at 8,400 feet above sea level, climbs somewhat higher, and descends to a sea level straightaway for the final ninety minutes or so. The advantage of the drive toward Guayaquil is that the precipitous ravine usually falls off on the left side of the two-lane road; the disadvantage is that you're headed downhill most of the way. Guard railings, few and far between, relieved a bit of my fear, except when the downhill section was bent outward or was simply broken off. For the better part of the first hour we followed a cattle truck, which moved only slightly faster than its cargo could have managed on its own.

The cattle turned off at Azogues, and we pushed on deep into the province of Cañar. The temperature dropped. I looked out the left side onto the clouds surrounding peaks nearby and distant. The thin air above the clouds in the Andes gave the sunlight colors unknown below. Only occasionally did our driver attempt a suicide squeeze—overtaking someone around a blind curve—and we settled into a quiet passage. Crude signs advertised local cheeses. Small piles of *toquilla* straw lay on the ground near doorless houses where women sat in the entrances weaving Panama hats. Julio, the driver, knew all the potholes and bumps on that road and managed to hit every one. Pepe, his helper—the driver's assistant is almost always a younger brother, son, or nephew—fidgeted with the radio until he found a distant station whose static muffled a brass band. We passed Cañari Indians heading home; in front the father, directly behind him his wife, behind her a passel of kids, and bringing up the rear a burro and a goat. Each party in the procession was connected to the one behind by a rope tied around the midsection. A dog yipped alongside.

We descended into the thick of the clouds and Julio downshifted. The white line down the center of the curving two-lane road was his only guide; even the *aerotaxi*'s hood ornament had disappeared into the clouds. After five minutes he slowed further and then stopped. Pepe walked through the *aerotaxi* collecting money. I nudged Horacio next to me. "What's this for?"

"We're at the shrine," he replied. "Each driver stops at this shrine along the way and leaves some money. It's their way of asking God's blessings for a safe journey." Often the saints are next to a police checkpoint so that the driver can make two payoffs at once. Offering insurance money to some saint required a gargantuan leap of faith, but if it would assure us a trip free of bus plunge, I wanted in. I coughed up a few *sucres*.

Pepe trotted across the road to leave our money at the shrine when suddenly a half-dozen Indian faces appeared out of the clouds pressing against the windows. "*¡Choclos! ¡Choclos! ¡Diez cada uno!*" They were selling sweet corn cooked with onion, cheese, and egg for slightly more than ten cents each. Two barefoot Indian women in felt hats and thick mud-stained ponchos slipped onto the bus and walked up and down the aisle. "*¡Choclos! ¡Choclos! ¡Nueve cada uno!*" The price had gone down some. Another vendor with a glazed look in her eyes and a baby in her arms rapped desperately on a window trying to get a passenger to open it. Her shrill voice seemed as distant as her eyes. Pepe returned, and the Indians withdrew into the Andean mist.

Bus drivers' assistants throughout Latin America display keen skills at hopping on and off moving buses, keeping track of which passenger is due how much change for his fare, pumping gas, climbing through a window to the roof to retrieve some freight before the bus stops, and changing blowouts. Pepe performed all these feats in the course of the run to Guayaquil, and excelled at hopping on the bus when it was already in second gear. Trotting apace of the bus, he first took a short skip on the ground to get the spring in his feet, then a short jump at a forty-five-degree angle calculated to land him on the first step while he grasped a metal bar next to the doorway. His motion appeared so fluid and effortless, he seemed to be simply stepping onto a bus in repose.

The right rear tire blew out on the southern edge of the town of Cañar. Julio pulled into an abandoned service station and Pepe had us back on the road within ten minutes. In more restful moments he sat on a makeshift seat between Julio and the door. The only job forbidden him was highway driving, and even then he was allowed to maneuver the bus around the terminals.

The ride down the western face of the Andes settled into a relatively peaceful journey once the tire was changed and the saint paid off. We went through long stretches where the only hint of life was an occasional *choza*, a straw-thatched hut, set back from the road. Valleys with streams and rivers flowing toward the Pacific held small towns. Our descent to sea level was practically complete and we entered a different climate, province, and culture. Bribing the saint had worked; we had passed the bus-plunge zone safely.

The air hung heavier, more humid, and warmer. Roadside vegetation grew more lush. Thick grass grew right up to roadside. Towns suddenly burst upon the highway—healthy, lively towns, active, jumping, noisy, uncaring. A church was just another building near the plaza, nothing more. Men and boys wore shorts, thongs, and torn T-shirts. Women and girls wore slacks or short, loose cotton dresses. Card tables were surrounded by men who looked like they'd sat there months on end encircled by a floating crowd of onlookers. Shot glasses of *puro* were constantly drained and refilled. Every structure was made of bamboo—split, dry, and aged. There was loud laughter, backslapping, gold-toothed grins, ass-pinching, life with few worries and less money. We had encountered our first *consteños*—people who live in the coastal region. Julio raced to Guayaquil on a road studded with potholes bigger than our *aerotaxi*. The tropics had begun.

CHAPTER FIVE

THE CITY OF MONKEYS

When you mention Guayaquil, the people of Quito snicker. *Monos*, monkeys, live there. Uncouth, sacrilegious, lazy, no modesty or commitment to family or God. They lack ambition, culture, and spirituality. Worse, they admit it without shame. Quito and Guayaquil have so little in common they appear as if on different planets. Guayaquil, whose industries produce most of the goods bought and process most of the food consumed in the country, is Ecuador's breadwinner. Most of the bread, however, winds up in government coffers in the capital city, and Guayaquil sees little benefit from its industrial output. Julio Estrada Ycaza, the executive director of the Province of Guaya Historic Archives, summed up the Guayaquil attitude toward Quiteños: "We live in the tropics; we work. They live in the mountains; they don't." Unattractive, hot, crowded, and constantly in motion, Guayaquil's strengths are abhorred by *serranos*—that is, mountain people, including Quiteños. On the coast, *monos* celebrate life with gaiety in the streets till dawn. In the mountains, *serranos* venerate death with solemnity in church till heaven. Until the bridge spanning the Guayas River was finally completed in the early 1960s, cars and trucks had to cross into Guayaquil on a ferryboat. Quiteños called the new bridge "the missing link."

Julio crossed over the missing link, guided the *aerotaxi* into the midst of three blocks of confusion, and parked in front of a hand-painted sign advertising regular departures for Cuenca. Instead of a central terminal, Guayaquil's interprovincial buses simply come and go from a crowded neighborhood near downtown, with *aerotaxis* and buses parked along every inch of curb, charging out of narrow alleys and filling all available pavement. Bus stations are little more than booths, with a dispatcher selling tickets and announcing departures.

Cabs and passenger cars squeeze through the lane between the buses, gleefully honking at each other. At every corner street vendors sell *cebiche*—chunks of marinated seafood floating in a lightly spiced liquid— and sugar and nail clippers and combs and magazines and cigarettes. A major port for South American ships, Guayaquil throbs as Ecuador's melting pot. It is a city in heat.

Rather than defend themselves against *serrano* accusations, Guayaquileños embrace them with humor. In *Vistazo*, humorist Tomás del Pelo challenged his readers to find "twenty-five tremendous mistakes" in a large cartoon of Guayaquil. Among the errors: city employees removing outdated political wall posters; a lady actually throwing garbage into a trash can; a taxi driver opening the door for a passenger; a working parking meter; a city inspector barring minors from an X-rated movie; a uniformed food vendor with a clean stand; a tavern shut down for being next to a school; a working pay telephone with its directory intact; students demonstrating for more classes; a hippie not smoking marijuana; a manned information booth with city maps and brochures; a radio serenading the streets with a Beethoven symphony.

I decided to leave for the fields of *toquilla* straw the next morning, and spend the rest of the day in Guayaquil hoping it would live up to its image. First I called on Edmundo Ward, at seventy-five a lifelong Guayaquileño and part owner of the city's main maternity hospital. His last name is an approximation of his family's original Lebanese name. He had commerce on his mind. "The Lebanese here are all bourgeois, and rabid capitalists," Ward said. "In Guayaquil, it seems everyone is selling something. Everything is sold here." We walked through the teeming central market district. Vendors filled the sidewalks for blocks and blocks hawking food, clothing, and furniture, candy, newspapers, and stereos, books, bedding, and themselves. "The Indians from the mountains come down here. They live twenty, sometimes thirty to a room in this area. This city has so little. On my way to work this morning I found an old friend begging on the streets. So I gave him all the money I had with me. Guayaquil is not a pretty city, but it has abundant activity. You can fix things by telephone if you know the right people. There was a time when I used to know everyone here. Now I feel as if I know no one. Here you can give affection, and take it too. If you can live with the chaos, you can make it here."

Ward gave a beggar a few *sucres*. "You need servants," he added. "Of course, there aren't as many servants as there were before. The women prefer to work in the factories." We had left the central market district and walked over toward the Malecón, the main street that runs along-side the river. Every block had Chinese and Lebanese restaurants.

"You see this factory? My father helped found it. It went broke a month ago. The manager was a crook. Our last mayor went to jail for the same reason. His fingernails were too long." The current mayor, a Lebanese, was a bombastic purist, colorful, unpredictable, and just a little maniacal. People called him a little dictator for his actions, unilateral and illegal, on behalf of the city. Once, to protest policies of the central government, he called for a citywide *paro*, a work stop-page, and enforced it with roving thugs. All transportation in and out of town was shut down (during which time Quiteños called the city "a cage full of monkeys"). "He's bad," Ward admitted. "He's not going to last." The next day the mayor announced plans to run for president in the next election. Months later, after he was charged with slandering the military and the central government, he surrep-titiously left the country.

We walked into an imposing apartment building and took the elevator to the seventh floor. "I have lunch with this family regularly. They're Lebanese and they are extremely wealthy. They own a major department store downtown. Life can be easy here. You'll see." The apartment was close enough to the Malecón so that the Río Guayas was in full view, but far enough so that the river's odor was not appar-ent. The spacious living room dripped with opulence. Wall-to-wall kitsch filled the living room. A cocker spaniel tap-danced across the marble floor. Cigarette ashes lay in sterling silver ashtrays. The women in the family talked of their latest shopping sprees in Miami and Europe. ("They spent fifty thousand dollars on a recent trip," Ward whispered.) No books were evident.

The midday meal, the main meal of the day, was delicious. Servants brought out five courses highlighted by seafood and veal. The coffee wasn't bad. "Those people don't understand me," Ward confided later, "but they give me affection. I have no family, and they think of me as one of them. I'm used to loneliness. I like it. I don't like domestic-ity. I would feel too limited. Ecuadoran women are too domesticated;

Lebanese women more so. Once you're in a Lebanese family, it absorbs all of you."

I asked Ward about the national rivalry between the coast and the *sierra*. "The Indians from the *sierra*—the ones who have initiative— they come here for work. They know we won't call them *indios brutos*," beastly Indians, "like they get called in Quito. No, we just ignore them. Of course, the roots of our nationalism are in the *sierra*."

As another *conseño* said of *serranos*, "The way they talk, it's like a bird chirping and twittering. They call us monkeys, we call them birds. When they drink, you know, they don't dance or laugh; they just drink until they fall down. Animals, animals. They don't bathe, you know."

"Have you noticed that there are no Guayaquileños in the air force?" Ward went on. "They don't want anything to do with it. They don't like uniforms. In Quito, everyone looks like a Christmas tree."

Women on the coast have a different personality from the *serranas* also. Taller, more lively and flirtatious, they look directly into men's eyes, instead of demurely glancing aside. Observed the Frenchman Laurent Saint-Criq in his 1875 book *Travels in South America: From the Pacific Ocean to the Atlantic Ocean*: "The female society of Guayaquil exceeds that of any other town in South America that I visited. Their private characters being as free from levity as their public demeanor is from prudery." I mentioned these perceptions to Ward. "It's true. No Guayaquileña would ever take a *serrano* from Quito for a husband. They think all *serranos* are hypocrites. Everything is different about them—the clothes they wear, the food they eat, the whole *ambiente*. There, they are closed."

We reached Ward's home, an apartment overlooking the Guayas River. It was filled with books of poetry, history, and philosophy. "I started writing poetry twelve years ago. I've published four books of poetry privately. This next one I hope to find a publisher for. I'm ready to invite criticism." He reached for his notebook. Writing poetry, he said, is *solitario y arduo*, solitary and arduous. "Here. This one is about Sitting Bull and Custer. Custer was a real bastard. Do you know a good translator?"

I left Ward to his poetry and went downtown to see Carlos Elías Barberán Loor at the finest Panama hat shop in the world. At times this obsession with Panama hats seemed to border on the ludicrous.

Weren't there better things to do than chase straw hats through South America? No. Through the Panama I could interpret the economic theories of Adam Smith and B. Traven, decipher Incan history, analyze United States foreign policy, and look at the First World from the outside in. I assured myself of all this on my way over to see Sr. Barberán.

Barberán, born in 1914, is known as the leading authority on Panamas, an opinion he himself is not reluctant to offer. Panamas of all qualities fill his store, from coarse and inexpensive Cuenca weaves to the very best from the province of Manabí. "My father was a *comisionista* in Manabí. That's where the most elegant hats have always come from, you know. My father lived in London between 1925 and 1930. Shortly after that we moved here to Guayaquil and opened up shop. I've been a one-man promoter of these hats for decades now. I developed the industry that now exists in Manabí."

Two towns in Manabí, Montecristi and Jipijapa (heepy-hahpa), have earned worldwide reputations over the years as the source of the finest Panamas. "I still get my best ones from Montecristi. Here's one that costs thirty-six thousand *sucres*," about three hundred dollars at the time. "It took eight months to weave." He held the hat up to the light and showed me the *vueltas*, the rings, which help determine the hat's value. "Here. How many do you count?" He handed me a hat weighing no more than an ounce, so smooth and soft you could easily pull it through a napkin ring. It rolled up into a cone, then opened back with nary a crease. So tight was the weave that very little light came through. I counted fourteen *vueltas*.

"Look again," Barberán counseled. "There are nineteen. Now for a hat like that, I paid the weaver twenty-six thousand *sucres*"—approximately two hundred forty dollars.

The payment was made in steps. "I pay twenty-five percent when the button and a little bit further are done; another quarter when the crown is complete, and the balance on completion. It looks very good on you."

Barberán placed a half-dozen different styles on my head, reeling off their names and the country where they are most popular. "I've been all over Central America selling hats, and also to Belgium, Switzerland, Portugal, Spain, England, France, and Germany. I was in your country last in 1978." In which country, I asked, do you find the largest heads?" "The United States! You Americans have the biggest heads in the world." He spoke with awe. "It's said the bigger the head, the smarter you are. Look at me!" Señor Barberán's head was small; there was no getting around that. He put his hands to the sides of his face to reinforce its narrow dimensions. "Now, this style looks good on me," he said, picking up a Panama with a small brim. "If you have a big face, though, get a hat with a wide brim."

We retreated to his desk, where he deplored the state of *fino* and *superfino* Montecristi Panamas. "There are ten families left in the entire Province of Manabí that make the extra-fine hats. They weave for three or four hours in the morning, or late at night. The rest of the day the sweat builds up on their fingers. Direct sunlight isn't good for the straw either. It gets too brittle to weave a proper *fino*. Before, there were a hundred families who could do it, and before that a thousand. But weavers don't get paid what the hats are worth, so now the people go into ranching or work on farms rather than make hats. In twenty years the weaving of the Montecristi *finos* will be all over." Barberán's sad prediction compelled me to add Montecristi to my itinerary before it was too late.

CHAPTER SIX

TOQUILLA SUNRISE

La Libertad lies on the coast seventy-five miles west of Guayaquil. The drive was flat, quick, and happily uneventful. We parked near the central market, a one-stop shopping center crowded with vendors selling fresh fruit, meat, vegetables, soft drinks, luggage, and a hundred more items. "The bus for Febres Cordero—where does it leave from?" I asked a lady selling onions. Over there, I was told, next to that ice cream stand. The only vehicles parked at the *heladería* were small pickup trucks. The bed of each pickup held two wooden benches under a low-slung metal shell with a couple of holes carved out. A boy of fifteen leaned against one of the trucks reading the morning newspaper. "Excuse me, could you tell me where to find the bus to Febres Cordero?" "This is it," he replied without looking up. "This pickup?" "*Sí.*" Laborers were loading cases of Coca-Cola on top of the shell. "We leave in forty-five minutes."

Four others joined me for the ride north. One was going all the way to Febres Cordero; the other three to Colonche. Uncomfortable and hot, the confines of the pickup grew even more so as passengers flagged us down to hop on. We started to overflow; the driver's helper and two passengers rode standing on the rear bumper. Little ventilation reached the front of the shell. We stopped every five minutes to let someone on or off. After ninety minutes most of the riders had left, and we remaining passengers could finally stretch out. "Which Febres Cordero do you want?" the driver's helper asked. "Lower or upper?" I guessed lower, hopped out, and paid the driver $1.10.

The note from Victor González in Cuenca had three names on it. I went from house to house asking for the men. The first one couldn't be found. The second was spending the day in La Libertad. The third was Ramírez, a man who could get me to the fields of the *toquilla* straw from which Panama hats are made. "Oh sure," a lady told me. "He's in upper Febres Cordero. He operates a *víveres*," a Third World 7-Eleven. "He should be behind the counter." The village of Febres Cordero was in one of the areas the U.S. State Department medical bulletin had warned about when I checked on possible diseases and their prevention. "If you're planning to travel outside the major cities, especially on the coast," a public-health nurse told me, "we suggest you get a tetanus-diphtheria shot, one for typhoid, and of course gamma globulin. Also, we recommend you take a Fansidar antimalaria pill once a week. Just in case." Every Thursday I popped my weekly malaria pill. It wouldn't prevent malaria from setting in, I was later told, but rather it controlled the symptoms.

Febres Cordero lies about twenty miles inland from the coast. The town itself was dry but not arid, hot but not sweltering. A dirt plaza at the center of town was surrounded by about ten houses and a church with a cement floor, cinder-block walls, and wooden benches. Its one light was fluorescent and hung over a cracked plaster Jesus. Kids from four to twenty used the plaza for a soccer field, careful to avoid the piglets who likewise played on it. Other homes lay farther back from the plaza. Most were made of split bamboo, often on wooden stilts, with ladders or stairways leading to the main floor. This prevented unwanted animals from wandering into the houses, gave some ventilation between the floor and the ground, and allowed rainwater to flow beneath the houses during torrential downpours rather than into them. The space between the floor and the ground was a storage area for drying *toquilla* straw. Piles of the stuff lay beneath one-room houses all over town. Except for the new straw itself, harvested within the previous seven days, everything in Febres Cordero appeared gray: people, hills, rocks, mules, calves, pigs, roads—all gray, gray as far as the eye could see. Year-old weather-beaten houses appeared as gray and old as twenty-year-old homes.

The coast wears a different cloak of poverty from the *sierra*. Clothing and shelter are cheaper, and fresh food is less expensive and more available. A primitive economy in towns as remote as this allows the richest man to earn perhaps ten or fifteen dollars more a month than the poorest. Febres Cordero had recently been wired into the nation's rural electrification grid, a fact advertised by the television antennas above some houses. Juan Ramírez, the third man on Victor González's list, had one on his house. When I called out his name he stuck his head out an open-air window and came down.

A dozen small children gathered as I explained my mission. Juan nodded, thought for a minute, and introduced me to some other men among the twenty or so people who had gathered around to gawk at the foreigner. A blue-shirted man about sixty took command. "In this town we not only harvest the straw," he intoned, "but we used to weave the hats as well. It was quite an industry here for a long time. We sent hats from here to Havana, Cuba." He tottered a bit and moved closer. His breath reeked of stale fermented sugarcane. The children laughed at his drunkenness. "Ecuador broke relations with Cuba in the year 1962. After that our market died and we stopped weaving hats. Our town has been poor ever since."

Two elderly women approached. "We used to make our living weaving the hats here," one said, "but since Cuba stopped buying we have had no way to support ourselves. We have no family here to care for us. We are alone."

Ecuador breaking relations with Cuba? Hadn't the CIA been instrumental in precipitating the split? In *Inside the Company: CIA Diary*, Philip Agee detailed the Agency's extensive undercover operations that drove an artificial wedge between Ecuador and Fidel. The divorce was part of a large-scale CIA effort to isolate Havana from hemispheric unity by creating friction between Cuba and all the other Latin American countries. Some of the fallout from that operation had landed here in Febres Cordero. United States foreign policy had unwittingly eliminated straw-hat weaving in a tiny South American village. The town has never recovered.

Juan invited me into his little store on the ground floor of his house. Daylight flooded the room as he opened the door, and a mouse scurried off the counter. One soft drink stood alone in the refrigerator. "The things I sell," Juan said, "are daily items for the people. It may look like these things stay here forever, but everything gets bought eventually. Everyone goes to La Libertad on market day to buy other things." On his shelves were the following: batteries, cigarettes, chewing gum, clothespins, oil, zippers, thread, notebooks, crackers, flour, noodles, lard, rice, canned tuna, aspirin, and 250-milligram tetracycline pills.

"You must be hungry. Would you like something to eat?" I bought the store's one soda and Juan reached for a dusty tuna can and crackers. "Here. You may have this." He picked up his machete and hacked open the tuna can. He poured its contents on a plate, added some stale crackers, and handed it to me. A crowd of fifty had gathered outside the little store to watch the gringo eat. Frankly, by this time I was getting tired of cute little barefoot kids following me around, but waving them off only heightened their curiosity.

"That man who was telling me about the straw industry here," I said to Juan. "What's his name? It came out all slurred when he told me."

"Who?" Juan answered. "Which one?"

"The drunkard in the blue shirt."

"Oh, him. That's my father."

"Well," I said, trying to recover, "he sure knows a great deal about straw."

"Oh, yes. It's his life. But he does drink a lot, doesn't he?"

Antonio, at eighteen the eldest of Juan's six children, drove a pickup between La Libertad and Febres Cordero for a living. He was scratching his head looking under his truck's hood. "Antonio will drive you out to the straw fields as soon as his truck is fixed," Juan said. "Domingo will go along too. He is a *pajero*," a straw cutter. By the time Antonio repaired his pickup and had poured some gas into the tank, half a dozen men had volunteered to come along. Two of them joined Domingo, Antonio, and me.

We drove off to the northwest, first zigzagging between houses, then onto an open dirt road. The ground was like soft clay. Some *pajeros* were coming in from the countryside, their day's work done by early afternoon. Pack mules walked alongside them, carrying bundles of *toquilla* straw strapped to their sides. They also carried bananas, mangoes, oranges, and, on each one, a small child. Soft of face, short of stature, and barefoot, the *pajeros* seemed gentle to an extreme. They called their machetes *piedras*, rocks, because that's what they were as hard as, but they treated them as if they were baby chicks. The *pajeros* waved as we drove by. The *toquilla* straw came in green shoots about a yard long and a quarter-inch in diameter. Each mule carried a load of forty shoots or so on each side.

We covered about four miles in twenty-five minutes, driving up and down some rolling hills. Pencil-thin cacti appeared near the road for the first few miles, but as we ascended they disappeared. The ground was getting wetter and the hills steeper. The truck had already slid on a short stretch of the road and Antonio feared worse slides ahead. He found a little space in which to turn the truck around, then parked in the middle of the road. Normally, Domingo said, the *pajeros* walk the entire distance. He, Antonio, and the other two left their shoes in the pickup and together we all walked deeper into the increasingly moist lowland rainforest.

"So it's the United States you're from?" one of the straw cutters asked as we walked along. "There was a man from this town who went to Holland. Tell me, is that near your country?" They talked of another friend who had just walked upon Mount Chimborazo, the volcano with a perpetual cap of snow. "On days like today we can see it from the path here," one *pajero* said, gesturing off in the distance to the right. "It's pretty, isn't it?"

We trudged another hour up and down steeper hills. Rain sprinkled lightly but steadily. Antagonistic mosquitoes joined us. The way grew more sloshy and humid. The muddy path was thick enough to suck the hind hoofs right off a bull. I took off my mud-caked sneakers and carried them over my shoulder. My feet had never looked whiter than they did against the black South American clay. Domingo noted my anxiety. "It's right over there," he said pointing his *piedra* in the distance. "We should be there soon."

Soon? What does soon mean to someone who walks barefoot three hours to work in the morning and back again at night? For all I knew he went home for lunch too. Soon? Distance and time are two of life's limitations that take on surreal qualities in Latin America. Dimensions mean little. Soon? It could mean today, tonight, tomorrow, by next week, or I'm not sure. Soon could be fifteen minutes or fifteen miles. The difference between soon and forever might be negligible. A few minutes later Domingo added: "We're getting closer."

Antonio, Domingo, and the others were not Indians. Neither were they Spanish, nor were they blacks from Esmeraldas, the city on the Pacific. They were *montuvios*, described by Rolf Blomberg in *Ecuador: Andean Mosaic* as *costeños* "in whom are fused the white, Indian and

Negro bloods in varying percentages. . . . In a hard and uneven struggle with the jungle, the climate, the wild beasts, the crawling reptiles, the treacherous rivers and his own fellow human beings, the 'montuvio' has managed to dominate the wilderness and has created sources of wealth of which he has but a minimum share. The 'montuvio' not only grows the cultivated tropical products, but exploits the wild jungle."

"There. Up ahead. That's where we're going." Domingo was more specific now. Every family in Febres Cordero is entitled to at least one *cuadra*, square, from which to harvest *toquilla* straw; the actual number of *cuadras* each family gets is determined annually at a community meeting. Domingo had worked his way up to ten *cuadras*, the maximum allowed. I had difficulty understanding just how big a *cuadra* is. At first Domingo indicated about ten yards square, then an area far larger. In any event, he seemed satisfied to have ten of them whatever their size.

We turned left off the wide path and walked into a lush sloping green forest with plants ten or twenty feet high. The mosquitoes from the trail followed us. After twenty yards Domingo stopped. "This is it. This is the *toquilla* straw." He clutched a slender green stalk rising ten feet off the ground with thin green leaves fanning out two to three feet from the center at the top. Other shoots had not yet flowered and remained tightly wrapped inside their green leaf casing. Those were the ones we wanted. Domingo took his machete in his right hand, held an unopened shoot in his left, and sliced it off where it connected to the trunk. He did it again with another shoot, and another and another. Antonio and the others took their machetes and did the same. In five minutes we had a pile of some fifty shoots. Here, eight miles down a back road from a village at the end of a dirt road in South America's tropical northwest, I had found the beginning of a Panama hat. Domingo sensed my pleasure. "Would you like an orange?" he asked. Without waiting for my nod he climbed a nearby tree and started tossing down its fruit.

Native South Americans had been weaving hats from *toquilla* straw long before the plant was christened *Carludovica palmata* by Hipólito Ruiz and José Pavón in the late eighteenth century. The two scientists, botanists at the Royal Garden of Madrid, traveled through Spanish America identifying and recording flora under appointment from King Carlos III of Spain. The name they gave the palm is a bilingual contraction of the Spanish and Latin names for his successor, Carlos IV, and his wife, Luisa. Although *Carludovica palmata* has been found as far north as Panama and as far south as Bolivia, nowhere are conditions better for its growth and regeneration than in Ecuador's coastal lowlands, where the fertile ground is moist but not saturated, where the wind carries the cooling air of the Humboldt Current in from the coast, and where taller plants shade it from the sun's direct rays. Each plant takes close to three years to reach full maturity. Although the plant grows wild for all practical purposes, when all the useful shoots have been cut from the main stalk, the seed, about the size of a baseball, is uprooted and replanted in shallow dirt nearby.

Domingo and the others stripped to the waist and used their shirts as sacks to carry the straw and fruit over their shoulders. They tied the bundles together at the top with strong narrow leaves found inside the greet shoots. Each sack weighed about fifty pounds.

We walked back through the hill country toward town in the afternoon heat. Along the way we passed a small one-room house on stilts, desolate in the countryside with a commanding view of the jungle. On the stairs leading up to the room sat a woman who smiled and waved as we walked by. In front lay a pile of *toquilla* straw, on top of which sat a large turkey. "Why do you find that so funny?" she asked when I laughed and pointed. "Well, we have a folk song in the United States about this very scene," I told her. "It's called 'El Pavo en La Paja.'" "Turkey in the Straw." I began to sing it, by which she was more startled than amused.

Each of the four men I walked with had completed primary school. "Most people here just go to the local school," Antonio said. "If you want to go beyond that," Antonio advised, "there is a school in Santa Elena," near La Libertad. "But it costs too much for most of us. Of those who go, some go back and forth every day. Others stay with relatives there during the week." The elementary school was in lower Febres Cordero. It had a corrugated tin roof and ancient wooden desks. The front of each desk supported a short bench providing a seat for the student in front. In all, twenty chairs were available for forty-five students. A nationalistic poem about Indians dominated the front wall. The final line read "I am Indian . . . I am American . . . and I speak Spanish!"

"I come out to the *toquillales*," the straw fields, "whenever I need money to feed my family," Domingo said. As a result, he comes three or four days a week, week after week, month after month, year after year.

In the nineteenth century, *toquilla* straw was exported from the Provinces of Guayas and Manabí. While this boosted the economy of the growers, it cut into the number of Ecuadoran hats sold abroad. Certainly if the raw straw were available in Venezuela, for example, the demand for finished hats from Ecuador would plummet; Venezuelans could weave their own. Ecuadoran weavers lobbied the national government, and in 1835, only a few years after Ecuador had broken away from Gran Colombia, the exporting of raw *toquilla* straw was outlawed. Demand for Ecuadoran hats increased and everyone was satisfied except the straw brokers, who managed to smuggle *toquilla* straw out of the country from secondary ports anyway. The ban on straw export was lifted in 1843 by President Juan José Flores, and *paja toquilla* went back on the international market. "Once someone brought some *toquilla* plants over to the Orient to see if they would grow in Japan or Formosa," an exporter told me. "It failed because of the climate. If it had worked over there, we'd all be in the gutter here."

We made it back to town while the sun still shone, and Domingo introduced me to his friend Demetrio. "When the straw comes in from the *toquillales*," Demetrio said, "The first thing we do is take the outer leaf off and shake it, like this." He picked up a shoot, peeled away the green leaf casing, and snapped it like a whip. What had been a straight stalk suddenly became like a light-colored horse's tail, with dozens of yard-long paper-thin sheaths hanging from a common stem. "Then we strip away the vein, the spine, and the coarse edge." With his fingernail Demetrio sliced into the plant, removing the unneeded parts. "After that, it goes in here." Demetrio led me (and my coterie of thirty kids) over to an oil drum filled with simmering water. A fire dug into the ground beneath the drum provided the heat. He tossed the opened palm fronds into the drum and let it boil for an hour or so. Every few minutes he stirred the straw soup with a long two-pronged pole. When the straw was completely boiled, he lifted it out with the pole and hung it on a clothesline to dry. Others dried the straw under their houses. The long strands shrivel up while they dry, each one forming a closed cylindrical fiber one yard long. Each individual fiber is then shredded into still narrower strands. The straw is boiled and dried again.

We leave the straw out to dry for the better part of a day," Demetrio said. "Sometimes longer. Then we bundle it all up into *bultos*"—the large sacks that make their way to the straw markets in Cuenca. "Every Monday we ship them by truck to Señor González, who has a warehouse in Guayaquil." According to González's note, he was paying about fifty dollars for each *bulto* that week. Sometimes he paid when he visited the straw harvesters, other times at his Guayaquil warehouse. Either way, his payment to the *pajeros* of Febres Cordero became the very first exchange of money on the long road to a Panama hat's final retail sale. Domingo had a *bulto* ready to ship to Señor González the following Monday.

La Libertad had the nearest public lodging, and the last truck for the day had left an hour earlier. The next one departed Febres Cordero at four-thirty in the morning, nine hours away. Juan invited me to have dinner and sleep at his house, which, from the outside, looked to be the fanciest place in town. Unlike most houses in Febres Cordero, cement had been used in its construction. Full steps with a railing, not just a ladder or a dugout plank, let to the second floor. He had electricity, lights, a refrigerator, and at least two rooms with a separate cooking area.

Antonio asked if I'd like to bathe before eating. At nightfall we hopped back into his truck and drove east a short distance until we reached a river. Antonio took off his clothes and waded into the thigh-deep water. I timidly followed. The water, cold and refreshing, flowed steadily but not fast. After a few minutes we heard a thunderous splash upriver. I froze and Antonio laughed. "Are you scared?" he asked. "Oh, a little," I admitted. "That was no animal, if that's what you think," he assured. "That was simply a big rock that fell into the river. We use the river for bathing and, farther down, for washing clothes. Most people come here when it's daylight out. Here's the soap. I'll leave the towel next to the river when I'm done."

Refreshed, I climbed the stairs to Juan's house. "Electricity has improved things here," he said when I asked about its recent arrival. "With electricity came hot plates, television, radio, and lights. Many of the women now use electric irons. Our health has improved because with refrigeration food can be preserved, and so can medicine. Before, we used wood stoves for all our cooking, charcoal irons, battery-operated radios, and candles. Have a seat. I think my *señora* has your dinner ready."

I sat at a wooden table that creaked when you breathed near it. The dining area looked out upon the plaza through an open-air window. (Except in a few cities, there is no other kind of window on the coast.) Juan's wife brought in a large tray, set it on the table, and hurriedly left. Although I dined alone, four sets of eyes kept sneaking glances at me from the adjoining rooms. Dinner consisted of a fried egg, rice, and a hard-boiled egg. I washed it down with an Inca Cola.

A half-hour later Juan and a relative walked in. "Well," he said, "perhaps you want to go to sleep. When the truck arrives at four-thirty, it will drive around the plaza a couple of times, honking. You'll hear it. I'll wake you then to make sure." I thanked him and looked around for a place to lie down. "Oh, we'll make your bed. Wait a minute."

They did make my bed. Literally. First they brought four boards out from the other room, followed by a couple of crossbeams. Then Juan got out a hammer and proceeded to nail the four boards to the crossbeams. A mattress no thicker than a heavy quilt was placed over the beams and a cloth was put on top of that. "Good night, *señor*," Juan said as he and the other man backed out of the newly christened guest room. "It is a pleasure to have you here." I turned off the light and looked out on the plaza. A few other lights in town were on, but they soon went off one by one. All was still. Even the piglets had gone to sleep.

I awoke on my own at four o'clock and packed my bag. I wasn't sure if leaving a token sum of money would be proper. Certainly Juan's family could use every *sucre* they could get even if they were, as they appeared, the richest in town. Would they consider a small gift from the foreigner insulting? I had no Miss Manners to consult on etiquette at the bottom of the Third World. Juan emerged from the adjoining room. We whispered our good-byes and I left some *sucres* under the empty bottle on the dinner table.

The truck arrived exactly on time, honked its way around the plaza, and picked me up. A couple more men hopped in at lower Febres Cordero, and we took off. The bench in back was as narrow and uneven as before. Whenever we hit a pothole or a bump, the top of my head scraped the roof of the metal shell; I adapted by sitting with my shoulders hunched together and my head bowed slightly. The predawn air was deceptively chilly, and I felt a cold threaten. Dozing became impossible. There was a time when I fancied travel like this incredibly romantic. Now I just considered it uncomfortable. We arrived just as La Libertad's marketplace opened its eyes for the day. I took the next bus back to Guayaquil.

CHAPTER SEVEN

REVOLUTION AND SEAFOOD

The hats to be made from Domingo's harvest, not yet even woven, had already been ordered by a company in the United States. Unknown to the *pajeros* in Febres Cordero, six months earlier, while the straw was in its final months of growth, a hat manufacturer in Texas had placed its annual purchase orders with several New York–based representatives of Cuenca exporters. The orders called for a variety of sizes and quality grades to meet the United States demand for dress, casual, and western hats made of straw. That year the Resistol Hat Company needed sixty thousand straw hat bodies. The company based its requisitions on projections in United States fashions, sales during recent years, availability from Ecuador, and its own capacity to prepare the hats for shipment to stores around the country.

Resistol started supplying haberdashers with hats in 1927, when it was known as Byer-Rolnick after its two founders: E. R. Byer, a Michigan jeweler who bankrolled Harry Rolnick, a hat maker. One of the company's brand names was Resistol. In the early 1960s Byer-Rolnick bought the Ecuadoran Panama Hat Company in New York, finishers of straw-hat bodies from Ecuador. With it came its supervisor, Irving Marin, the premier Panama hat craftsman in the United States. "He had such a keen eye for straw hats and how to treat them in the plant," a co-worker said of him. "We'd had seventy-two thousand straw-hat bodies in the warehouse for years. Everyone wanted to throw them out, but Irving turned them from junk into dollars. He could make chicken soup out of garbage."

Byer-Rolnick was eventually swallowed by Koret, a California clothing manufacturer, but retained its own identity and headquarters in Garland, a suburb of Dallas. In 1979 it assumed the name of its best-known brand, Resistol.

Among the California forty-niners, the dreamers who first popularized Ecuadoran straw hats in the United States, was a young immigrant from Bavaria named Levi Strauss. In 1980, the San Francisco–based jeanswear company bearing his name took over Koracorp Industries, the new name for Resistol's owners. The straw that Domingo cut near Febres Cordero and shipped to Victor González's warehouse in Guayaquil was now entering the pipeline to be handled by the largest apparel manufacturing firm in the world.

No one knows who first developed the idea of processing shoots from the *toquilla* plant to weave into natural fiber hats, or in which century this triumphant marriage of form and function took place. A primitive but inexorable process simply occurred, much as in evolution: there was a need for lightweight protection from the sun, and *toquilla* was a handy plant to use. Where did they learn to open up the *toquilla* shoot, to boil it, to strip it into thin strands, and to style the weave so that the hat would fit the head? Trial and error. Natural selection. Other plants, no doubt, were used and rejected until the right fiber and the right process went hand in hand.

From *Straw Hats—Their History and Manufacture*, by Harry Inwards, London, 1922: "Claims are made that in the Province of Manabi, a native named Francisco Delgado first made a Panama hat about 300 years ago. The very Spanish name for a native evokes a suspicion that the date given was the first *Spanish* record . . . for it is most probably that the making of grass fibre hats in the Western Hemisphere was . . . of the most remote antiquity."

Inwards was probably right. When the conquistadors first wandered through Manabí, they saw people wearing a strange headdress shaped like vampire wings. Perhaps to test the Spaniard's gullibility, the natives said that the hats were woven from actual vampire skin. With these hats the Spaniards protected themselves from the sun, and because the hats were woven so tightly, they would carry water in them as well. Later the Spanish learned they had been fooled. The headdress was made from a locally grown light fiber.

The most delicate of the woven headdresses were worn by women like a linen handkerchief on their heads or around their necks. Men wore them with feathers sticking out or with bands around them. They were called *toquillas*, from the Spanish *toca*, or headdress. In the seventeenth and eighteenth centuries the hats made in Manabí gained wider distribution. Craftsmen were sent south from Manabí to Guayaquil and Peru to teach hat making. The hats and *toquilla* straw were sold as far inland as Cuenca. A small number were shipped to the United States, where, according to one account, "it was believed that they were fruit from the *paja toquilla* tree, and that these hats hung from its branches. One had only to pick them when they had turned white in color, a sign that they were ripe."

In 1834 rival officers vied for power within the new republic. One faction, attempting to control Manabí, ordered that all the Panama hats in the towns of Montecristi and Jipijapa be collected to raise money. The hats were hidden from the plunderers and smuggled out to Peru and Colombia. Montecristi, Manabí's main straw-weaving town, shipped its hats through Guayaquil, 120 miles south, and Manta, 12 miles north. In 1849, at the height of the California gold rush, Ecuador exported more than 220,000 straw hats.

Manta today is a lively port town busy with sailors and fishermen. Extensive beaches, an archaeological museum, and boating attract visitors. Playing on the beach one day were new recruits from California for the Summer Institute of Linguistics, the missionaries known in the United States as the Wyckliff Translators. The young group was staying at a nearby retreat. They acted like they had just gotten off the boat. "We're the ones who translate the Bible into native tongues," one said. "A couple of our people got killed in, where was it, Peru? Colombia? Anyway, we figured we'd fatten up and get a good tan before we got it too." "Yeah," his sidekick added, "so the pictures of our corpses will look good."

At Manta's museum schoolchildren marveled at a display illuminating life in the Valdivian period, more than 1500 years BC. At the yacht club, a bedraggled boat captain walked up to the table where I drank Pilsener with a few members. The captain, from Los Angeles, said he was on his way down the Pacific Coast to the southern tip of South America. "Mind if I dock at your club for a couple of days?" The yachtsmen looked at him, then at his schooner, then at each other. "Sure," they replied. "Everyone else does."

Everybody in town advised me to visit Fernando Zevallos Marzumillaga. He knows more about the history of Manabí than anyone. Just walk up to his door.

Don Fernando received me cordially. In his eighties, he was frail of body but keen of mind. Unfortunately, I couldn't understand his Spanish. Like many *costeños*, he eliminated most *s*'s and swallowed the last syllable of most words. I prayed for *s*-less endings and three-syllable words, and yearned for the clear Castilian of the *sierra*. Don Fernando's son Alejandro, fifty years old, repeated his father's words in more accessible Spanish. "I have some things you might like to see," Don Fernando said. "First, so you will know who I am, this is my card."

FERNANDO ZEVALLOS MARZUMILLAGA

Titulado y Condecorado Benemérito de Montecristi, Miembro de la Casa de la Cultura del Ecuador, de Unión Nacional de Periodistas del Ecuador, del Centro Cultural "Manta", del Patronato Histórico "Guayaquil", Asesor Histórico del Concejo de Manta, Emérito del Instituto Ecuatoriano del Seguro Social, Miembro de Honor de la Sociedad Jurídico-Literaria de Manabí y Miembro Asesor de la Comisión de Límites del Consejo Provincial de Manabí, Colaborador del Mercurio de Manta, La Provincia y Diario Ecuador de Portoviejo.

Titled and Decorated Meritorious Benefactor of Montecristi, Member of the Ecuadoran House of Culture, of the Ecuadoran National Union of Journalists, of the Manta Cultural Center, of the Guayaquil Historical Foundation, Historical Adviser to the Manta Council, Emeritus Member of the Ecuadoran Social Security Institute, Honorary Member of the Boundary Commission of the Provincial Council of Manabí, Contributor to the *Manta Mercurio*, *La Provincia*, and the *Diario Ecuador of Portoviejo*.

"I have here some old clippings. Take a look." From his files he had retrieved fifty-year-old brochures about Montecristi, articles about the heyday of Panama hats, and mementos of General Eloy Alfaro, Manabí's favorite son. Alfaro, born in Montecristi in 1842, led the Liberal Revolution, which brought a measure of enlightenment to the country when he became its ruler in 1895. *Costeños* have traditionally had more progressive ideas than people from the interior, since ships docking in port towns unload news and ideas as well as goods from the outside world. Prior to Alfaro's regimes—he held office twice—a Roman Catholic theocracy ruled. Only Roman Catholics could vote, hold office, or teach. The Liberal Revolution restricted the influence of the Church, brought about separation of Church and State, instituted secular public education, and allowed for civil marriage and divorce. Church land became state land. For this Alfaro is a national hero, revered in the tradition of Washington and Lincoln.

Alfaro's father, Manuel, and later Eloy himself, made a good living exporting Ecuadoran products to Panama, especially *toquilla* straw hats. Manuel, in fact, is often heralded as the first of the major hat exporters. In the Zevallos house hangs a color drawing of Eloy Alfaro, with mountains in the background. Don Fernando showed me a postcard of Alfaro brandishing his sword aboard a steamer at the 1884 battle of Jaramijó, near Manta. Sixty-year-old sheet music sang the praises of the Liberal Party, whose beginnings the Alfaro family helped finance. A bust of John F. Kennedy sat next to the lamp. A 1909 German typewriter rested on a table. Its keys were to the left and right side of the carriage rather than in front of it. It had no keys for punctuation. Don Fernando had used it until recently.

He recited local history with the passion of a historian credentialed by devotion to his subject and love of its people. "*Toquilla* straw hats have covered the heads of Napoleon of France, Edward VII and George V of England, and Hoover and Roosevelt of the United States." I told him that every United States president since Grover Cleveland has been given a Panama by the government of Ecuador. He arched his eyebrows, inserting that fact into his history of the region.

Reading up on the country's history, I had developed a theory I wanted to try out. "*Oiga*, Don Fernando," listen. "If the Alfaro family supported Eloy's political activities"—Zevallos nodded slowly—"and its money was made, in part, from exporting *toquilla* straw hats"—he nodded again—"then Panama hats are at least partially responsible for Ecuador's great Liberal Revolution. Isn't that so?" Zevallos smiled benignly.

His son was anxious to continue the discussion. He delighted in speaking with a foreigner in his house, teaching about his homeland and talking about travel. He poured me some weak instant coffee. I asked if he knew of the missionary retreat I'd been told about earlier. "Well, I've heard of it," he replied. "But tell me—why do they come?" He ticked them off on his fingers. "There are Mormons, Seventh Day Adventists, Jehovah's Witnesses—and Catholics! This country is ninety-eight percent Catholic and still they send missionaries." His face took on an air of incredulity. "Are they trying to capture the other two percent? And these hippies we see, why do they come? Why do they act the way they do?" Perplexity now colored his face. "Their dirty long hair! Is it really true they're from the families of the rich?"

Alejandro pulled out a picture album from a 1973 visit to the United States. "I had a wonderful time in your country. I went to the Macy's Thanksgiving Day parade. Here I am with the other members of the Dinosaur Club—that's an international group I belong to. I was their guest. Here I am with Snoopy." He showed off photographs of parade floats, marchers, and of himself with smiling New York City policemen. Picture postcards of Chinatown, the Rockefeller Center skating rink, and the San Francisco Bay Bridge filled the next few pages. "I've never been to San Francisco," he admitted. "I just like the picture. I sent a Montecristi *fino* to the head of the Dinosaur Club in New York when I got home."

Together we walked downhill to the center of town. I had expressed some interest in going to Jaramijó, the town where the legendary Alfaro had fought. "It's a primitive fishing village, but you'll like it. Over there." He pointed to a main street. "That's where you catch the bus. It goes by the park with a statue of John F. Kennedy."

A half-hour later I was ordering lunch at the Bar Picantería Embajador in Jaramijó, an open-air restaurant on the beach looking out at the Pacific Ocean. The Embajador was covered with a tin roof from which hung a bare light bulb. To reach the bathroom I passed through the town's schoolroom, which was behind the kitchen. Fishermen were coming in from the Pacific with the morning's catch, rolled their old wooden boats up the beach at low tide over short bamboo logs. Children scrambled around each boat helping unload the fish into rubber buckets and plastic bags. Some carried fish away in their hands. A World Cup soccer match between Germany and France blared out over the radio. Among the boats on the beach a scrawny woman sat cross-legged, waving her arms wildly at the incoming fleet as if conducting a symphony at the finale of the last movement. "She's crazy," a teenager said, "but we're used to her. She's here every day."

Naval officers from Manta dined a few tables away with their girl-friends. An elderly lady walked up offering seashells for twenty *sucres* each, about thirty cents. Barefoot, she stood a few inches shy of five feet tall. "Twenty *sucres?* Why, I could walk out there and find some for free," I countered. "Yes, but not like these." Her shells possessed no special qualities, but her face wore a mask of urgent desperation. "OK," I said. "Ten apiece. I'll buy a couple." She beamed. Pelicans, dogs, and seagulls came by in groups of two. The seashell lady hovered around my table throughout lunch. Steamed fresh lobster cost three dollars.

Three buses leave Manta for Montecristi every hour, passing coffee-processing factories and dry scrub brush along the way. In Montecristi I hoped to find some weavers who saw that their precious heritage was bought for a few *sucres* and sold for lots of dollars; that they were at the poor end of an increasingly profitable chain in which each person made more and more money off their original labor. I couldn't explain the *Wealth of Nations* to them, or theories of productivity and profit, but I longed to see awareness beyond a shoulder shrug. Don Fernando nodded when I mentioned this to him earlier at his home in Manta. "I've got just the thing for you." He rummaged through his files and came up with a 1974 booklet promoting Montecristi. He turned to a page with a poem whose author is identified as Lupi.

El Sombrero de Montecristi

A wondrous fiber, known
To the world under an assumed name;
Artful propaganda
Of poorly paid, silent labor.

The peacocking of pampered people;
A well-spring, fertile and enduring,
Of misfortune to the poor
And extravagance of the wealthy.

A fine warp, a painstaking marvel
That transforms the straw
Into exquisite high fashion.

The holocaust of a people who naïvely
Sponsor a pitiful way of life,
Bound into sheaves of trampled misery.

CHAPTER EIGHT

MONTECRISTI FINO

Throughout Latin America, generals, poets, and revolutions are honored with streets named for their anniversaries. Between Tijuana and Cape Horn, I am convinced, there is a street named for each day of the year. My bus ride ended on Ninth of July Street, a few blocks from Montecristi's main plaza. No one I asked in Montecristi seemed to know what event the name of their main street commemorates, or at least no two people agreed on its antecedent.

The town's few hundred houses are standard coastal buildings: raised off the ground, made of graying split bamboo, lacking electricity and water, many without doors in their doorways, most with nothing in the windows. The ground resembled the ocean floor.

Within moments of arriving I was surrounded by half a dozen boys. "Mister! Panama hats?" they squealed, exhausting their English vocabulary. "Panama hats!" Each one wanted to drag me off to his family's house or store to look at hats for sale.

Hats exported from Montecristi sell for hundreds of dollars in the United States and Europe. In an area where once virtually every household produced the highest quality hats, the number of weavers has slowly but irreversibly diminished. This scarcity has driven prices up at the receiving retail end, but in Montecristi the weavers' income has not made a commensurate rise. Outshining the hats produced in Cuenca, Montecristis are virtual silken treasures, sleek and supple, each one an admirable example of delicate handicraft.

"Take me to the home of Rosendo Delgado," I said to the kids who had met me at the bus. "Sure," they said in unison. "Follow us." Delgado's name had been given to me as a highly respected exporter of fine Panamas. We walked up Ninth of July Street past the town plaza and turned left at the church. Stores offered hats and furniture made

of a sturdier straw, but few had customers inside. A statue honoring
Mother's Day had been erected by the side of the road. "*Madre*," said
the inscription, "*símbolo y blazon de homenaje perpetuo.*" Mother—sym-
bol and blazon of perpetual homage. A block farther we crossed John
F. Kennedy Street, and then on Rocafuerte Street the boys pointed to
the corner house. "He lives there."

Don Rosendo Delgado looked out an upstairs window. "Come on
up, come on up." His hair was jet-black, his eyes alert, and his mouth
still had many of its teeth. He appeared to be in his fifties and wore
a loose shirt and baggy pants. He nodded his head thoughtfully as
I explained my quest. "Well, there's really nothing to it. The weavers
from the countryside come here with the hats, and we finish them.
Then I sell them."

Two other men sat in the living room with him, each with a small
bowl of water beside his chair. They held Panamas about ninety-
five percent complete. One knotted the straws on a hat's outer brim
together, giving it a smooth edge. The other trimmed his hat's straw
fringe, reducing its length from six inches to a quarter inch. The hat
got a haircut better than his own. Now and then each would hold a
hat up to the light looking for imperfections—a gap in the weave, a
discoloration, a slight hole, or loose or broken straws. Both men wore
a couple of Panamas, using their heads as inventory control. They kept
all the hats away from the direct sunlight, and constantly dipped their
fingers into the water to keep the straw moist. Water runs through
the faucets of Montecristi for two hours every day—that is, in homes
equipped with faucets. A truck selling water by the pailful wends its
way through town irregularly. Panama hats, contrary to popular myth,
are not woven under water.

On a wall map Delgado pointed out where the weavers live who
bring him hats, and where their straw grows. "The best straw for this
area comes from Manglaralto and Olón," he said. "I get hats from all
over—from Pila, Tres Bajo de la Palma, and Las Pampas. Some weavers are lucky. Straw grows near their houses so they don't have to buy
it at market." At least I think that's what he said, for Delgado's Spanish
was even harder to comprehend than Fernando Zevallos's. He spoke as
if he held marbles in his mouth. "*Más o menos*"—more or less—came
out "*maomay.*" He was on a low-consonant diet, feasting on vowels.

Delgado's father had been in the same business, and his father before him and his before him. Could Francisco Delgado, the early seventeenth-century Panama hat entrepreneur in Montecristi, have been related? "Well, yes, he could have been. We don't know. There are lots of Delgados in this area. Lots. At one time or another we've all had relatives in the hat trade. That's what we do."

Don Rosendo's younger brother Carlos dropped by. Carlos taught school. "I teach a little about the area. Do you know how old these are?" He took two objects off a shelf—a broken bowl and a shard of some pottery. "They were made by people who lived here many centuries ago. We find lots of pre-Columbian pottery in this area."

A Mercedes Benz pulled up out front and honked. "It's for you," Carlos told his brother as he glanced out the window. "Someone from Guayaquil." Rosendo loped down the stairs. The Guayaquileño introduced four well-dressed visitors from Spain, happy to have completed their dusty trip north. They talked a bit, and Delgado unlocked his ground-floor *bodega*. Inside, stacked against the walls, on chairs and tables, Delgado kept hundreds of high-quality Panamas. He showed the Spaniards different styles— ventilated, tight weave, wide brim, high crown, ladies' fashions, and *óptimos*. The Spaniards inspected them carefully, setting aside the ones they wanted. Delgado announced his price; they suggested a lower price for a higher quantity, and back and forth it went on the wooden sidewalk, these well-manicured Europeans speaking elegant Castilian negotiating with the slightly unkempt *mestizo* speaking his slurred Spanish. The Spaniards did their calculations in their heads; Delgado did his on brown wrapping paper. Soon they reached an accord. "Would you like them in boxes?" They would. With a flourish, Don Rosendo Delgado, expert hat finisher and exporter of some of the finest Panama hats in Ecuador, folded each hat in half, rolled it up into a tight cone, sealed it in paper, and ceremoniously placed it in a cozy balsa-wood box. Everyone smiled and shook hands. The Spaniards piled back into the Mercedes and Don Rosendo lumbered back upstairs. The little boys who had led me to Delgado's place watched quietly the whole time.

The next day I returned to Montecristi. When I hopped off the bus and heard a band playing the U.S. Marine Corps song, "*From the halls of Montezu-u-ma . . . ,"* I froze. Had they invaded? The music, it turned out, came from a nine-piece band that zigzagged its way through the town's ten streets in every conceivable geometric pattern for an hour. The band alternated between the Ecuadoran national anthem and the Marine song. Incessant fireworks punctuated the music. During a military coup in the early 1970s, a Quito radio station, between breathless news bulletins from the front, alternated the national anthem with "There's No Business Like Show Business." "It's too bad you weren't here during our last coup," a government secretary in the capital said. "They're really a lot of fun. While the *palacio* was being attacked, everyone else was over at the big soccer game at the stadium. Our coups, they're so—they're so"—her mind grappled for the right word—"they're so folkloric."

A parade five-hundred strong followed the musicians. Women wore their finest dresses, many with sashes saying DAMA DE HONOR. Men showed off their best suits; their sashes announced their government rank. When I asked what everyone was celebrating, I was told, "Why it's a civic *fiesta*!"

The civic *fiesta* came to a rest next to the plaza. An elegantly dressed lad of eighteen, sitting astride a horse, spoke to the throng. "In this time of economic crisis"—the *sucre* had been devaluating wildly that week—"we honor . . ." His words were lost to indiscriminate fireworks and a faulty loudspeaker. The formalities dispensed with, the townspeople milled about waiting for Los Amigos del Ritmo de Jaramijó, a five-piece dance band, to set up in an open-air storefront on Ninth of July Street. Crepe paper, ribbons, and paper globes decorated the setting.

A block away, Arte Típico was just opening for the day. Run by two sisters known as the gypsy ladies for their gaudy appearance, the store sold stylish Panamas and other straw products to tourists. On one counter they displayed a photograph of themselves giving a Panama hat to Sheik Yamani of Saudi Arabia at an OPEC meeting in Ecuador. A museum highlighting the area's pre-Columbian history filled the back of the store. As in the other hat outlets in town, the Panamas at Arte Típico came rolled up in boxes made by Jorge Lucas, a Montecristi carpenter who turned sheets of waste balsa into three dozen boxes daily. Each box had the Ecuadoran flag stenciled on top, along with the words *Montecristi Fino*. Lucas sold them to retailers for thirty-five cents each.

In the 1970s, when more and more *campesinos* were finding hat weaving less and less profitable, a government program promoted the weaving of smaller items that required less time and brought in marginally more money. Among the straw items made of *toquilla* and other fibers now regularly turned out are placemats, baskets, and handbags, plant holders, dolls, and Christmas tree ornaments. Because these curios generate a higher income, fewer craftsmen bother with Panama hats. Rosendo Delgado mourned the loss of his best weavers who had ceased making *sombreros de paja toquilla*.

CHAPTER NINE

THE VISITING JUDGE

Pre-Columbian artifacts adorned every *costeña* home, but only at the coastal village of Salango were they methodically mined. An archaeological dig was taking place there, run by the central government and staffed by a few Ecuadorans and many workers from Europe and the United States. I went first to Jipijapa to board a bus for Puerto López, where the Salango expedition maintained a house.

According to a gringo I had met in Quito, a well-traveled veteran of South America's third-class buses and threadbare flophouses, Jipijapa ranks among the ugliest towns south of the Equator. He did not exaggerate. The bus pulled up to the plaza surrounded by the best Jipijapa had to offer: two-story buildings whose upper balconies sagged under the weight of their years, walls from which all the paint had peeled decades ago, stores that dared you to enter, restaurants that repulsed the hungriest traveler. This was a town famous for its Panama hats? I could find none anywhere. Its reputation was ancient history. I ducked into a back alley to relieve myself before boarding the bus for Puerto López. My discretion was unnecessary in Jipijapa, for when I returned to the plaza the driver was doing the same on the side of his bus. One day the Quito newspaper reported that some men in Guayaquil had been fined five dollars each for publicly urinating. Erasing Ecuador's 7.5-billion-dollar foreign debt suddenly seemed very easy.

Very willing to depart Jipijapa, I hopped on a sixty-cent bus headed west to Puerto López. Its bumper sticker read GOD WATCHES OVER MY BUS, the irony of which had been demonstrated the previous week. Although the route to Puerto López lacks ravines and gorges, the same bus had blown a tire and careened off the road. Most of its passengers required medical treatment.

Puerto López is a town full of fishing boats and nets, front-porch hammocks, and dogs, kids, and pigs all playing near each other. Next to an open-air barbershop, the local movie theater—thirty folding chairs surrounded by four see-through walls—advertised a kung fu movie. The town of three thousand showed a measure of prosperity: Houses were constructed of brick in addition to bamboo. Many had outdoor staircases with railings, metal grills over the windows, and second-story balconies overlooking the ocean. Local businessmen walked around in swimming trunks and open shirts. Workers were installing a new electrical transformer. A television set rested precariously on a porch railing as a crowd gathered around to watch test patterns from Guayaquil. Puerto López, one of the viewers volunteered, even had a red-light district of sorts. An afternoon breeze blew through some palm trees on the beach. A wooden bench faced the South Pacific. A Schwinn bicycle rested against it.

When I got off the bus a man had instructed me to go to Carmita's, a restaurant two blocks away on the beach. "Why?" I asked.

"Aren't you here to see the Peace Corps volunteer?"

This was not the first time I had alighted from a bus in a small town to be met by the suggestion that I visit the local Peace Corps contingent. For what other conceivable reason would a gringo come to such a place?

Since 1962, when the Peace Corps sent its first trainees overseas, Ecuador has admitted an uninterrupted flow of volunteers—more than three thousand of them within the agency's first quarter century. Occasionally helpful and innovative, sometimes ineffectual, they have become familiar to remote villagers and big-city dwellers alike. More than two hundred volunteers were scattered around the country. One was attached to the archaeological dig nearby, and she, along with the others from the site, gathered at Carmita's after work every day for cold beer and cheap seafood. Carmita said they'd show up between five and six o'clock.

I wandered back to the main street, drawn by the sound of a brass band and a noisy crowd, and rounded the corner just in time to see hundreds of people parade by. The whole town, it seemed, was out celebrating the birthday of the Puerto López high school. Students wore homemade costumes. Each group in the parade

adopted a different personality. Bands honked down the streets—
El Trío was one, The Eight Ponchos another. A third, consisting of
a drum, guitar, and tin horn, wore absurd wigs at forty-five-degree
angles to their foreheads. "Los Hippys de Puerto López" was the
next bunch, twelve boys affecting wigs, beards, and baggy clothes.
Knapsacks hung on their backs. Carrying fake cameras, they ran over
to the side pointing their lenses at the faces of onlookers. In retreat,
they mimicked marijuana smokers, cheerful and loony. A pickup
truck cruised behind them, broadcasting loud music from its bed
for a gaggle of dancing clowns who twisted down Main Street. Pom-
pom girls sashayed over to the onlookers, giggling at their friends.
Girls danced with girls, boys with boys. One of the "hippys" ran over
and handed me a popsicle.

"Excuse me," a man said, approaching. "Are you a visitor here?" He
introduced himself as César Aguilar, director of the school celebrating its anniversary. "We have two hundred fifty students and eleven
teachers at Colegio Provincial de Manabí," Aguilar told me. "Our students are twelve to sixteen years old. That class there"—some teenagers dressed in sailor outfits marched by, wearing imitation Panama
hats made of paper—"those are our oldest." He paused to wave to a
blackface chain gang under the whip of the local police, who stumbled
all over themselves. The police chief wore an evil mustache. "And these,
we're very proud of them." More students pranced by, this time dressed
as Colombians in two-tone straw hats and calf-length pants. A teacher
holding a cassette machine playing Colombian music walked on the
sidelines in step with the group.

"Would you like to be a judge?" Aguilar asked. "We need another
one. Each judge selects the group he thinks is best in the parade. We'd
be honored to have you. When the parade is over, come over to my
office and vote for your favorite group."

Word spread fast among the students. I paced the sidelines, catch-
ing each group at least twice. Everyone who passed me put on a special
show. Musicians played louder, dancers stepped higher, clowns acted
loonier. A striking fifteen-year-old in black stiletto heels, a white sailor
outfit, and a Panama hat stared straight at me and smiled mischie-
vously each time she marched by. This miserable little village by the sea
seemed an inviting place to stay.

In the end I voted for the high-stepping Grupo Folklórico Consteño, as did two of the other four judges. When the winning group was announced at the school dance that night, my high-heeled sailor shot me a pout sad enough to melt the ice atop Mount Chimborazo. I kicked myself for not choosing her group. I had obviously come from a country that takes voting far too seriously.

CHAPTER TEN

CARMITA'S PEACE CORPS BAR AND GRILL

Half a dozen workers from the dig at Salango pulled up at Carmita Yanchapaxi's open-air restaurant for happy hour. King-size bottles of cold beer were plunked on the table as the sun began its slow descent beyond the Pacific Ocean. Carmita's menu hung from the ceiling, each entrée inscribed on a separate wooden plaque. We had a choice of meat, lobster, soup, fish, snails, crayfish, and marinated seafood. When a sea breeze blew into Carmita's, the snails clacked against the lobster and the crayfish against the meat. I ordered a shot of Cristal, the distilled sugarcane known for its fearsome potency, but Carmita suggested Caña Manabita instead. "It's better than Cristal," she boasted. "It's made here in Manabí Province. We're very proud of it. I sell it by the shot or by the bottle." She played *Zorba the Greek* on her cassette deck as a boy bicycled by hawking bananas and oranges. Two young *campesinos* on donkeys followed. "Here, Lassie!" Carmita called to a nearby dog. "I've got some scraps for you." Half the mutts in town were named Lassie, as far as I could tell. The dogs of Puerto López, far friendlier and less threatening than most Latin American dogs, passed their time copulating in the streets, oblivious to the kids playing soccer around them.

Just as the workers from the Salango dig began their second round of beer, a dusty jeep pulled up and Presley Norton, a portly man in a flak jacket, climbed out. Norton, an Ecuadoran-born anthropologist schooled in the English-speaking world, was the project director. His arrival was welcomed not only so his staff could brief him on activities and discoveries made since he left a few days earlier but because he brought their mail from a post-office box in Quito. Unwinding from a day that had taken him by air from Quito to Guayaquil, then third-class bus and jeep up the coast, Norton handed out envelopes from Europe and the States. Two contained cassette tapes; one of David Bowie, the other, Vivaldi. "They call this town the Acapulco of Ecuador," a Scandinavian worker said. "There's even an Acapulco Restaurant here. Is Acapulco as primitive as this?" "No, but it's a darn sight more expensive," Norton replied.

The Peace Corps worker, a cultural anthropologist by title, said she worked in community development acting as liaison between the Salango crew and the town. What this appeared to mean was that she was the first to arrive at Carmita's and the last to leave. "This place first opened in 1966," she said. "Carmita lives above the restaurant with her relatives. If there's one thing we've learned, it's that you don't cross her. One night we went to that place on the beach across the road, and Carmita snubbed us for a long time. We told her we were just trying out the competition to see how much better her food was, but she didn't believe us."

Smuggling, the occupation common to coastal villages in every hemisphere and under all governments, plays a role in the economy of Puerto López. "Once or twice a week a boat anchors offshore just north of town," one observer said. "They don't carry drugs, although they do come from Colombia. They unload electronic consumer goods instead. We can tell when there's a delivery because the local power always goes out then. It ensures a safe and worry-free landing. They say Carmita carries a revolver strapped to her thigh."

By the time the next round came we had just finished analyzing British writers, having earlier dispensed with Russian novelists and Argentine poets. My theory that Panama hats were responsible for Ecuador's great Liberal Revolution met polite approval. We were planning to divvy up the world's resources in gold bullion when I told Norton of my fascination with Latin American buses. "You know," he said, "the wife of Velasco Ibarra," five times president of Ecuador between 1933 and 1972, "died in Buenos Aires where they lived in exile. She was trying to get on a crowded bus after it had started moving and missed the step. Velasco himself died six months later. They said it was from a broken heart."

A middle-aged woman from the United States Midwest nodded, absorbing every tidbit of local international lore. She occupied the floating Earthwatch position, reserved for whoever had the interest to spend a few weeks helping out around the site and the money to pay for the privilege. From its office outside Boston, Earthwatch offers "learning vacations" to the public. People work for a few weeks alongside archaeologists, astronomers, anthropologists, art historians, biologists, and others at some eighty sites on every continent, paying more than a thousand dollars each for the privilege. One Earthwatcher I'd met a few weeks earlier spent fourteen days on the Galápagos Islands watching turtles defecate. "The Earthwatcher we have now is useful," Norton allowed, "but we've had problems with some of them. Most have no experience and false expectations. Some just stand around and watch like it's a spectator sport. A number of them get frustrated. Overall our experience has been good, but since each one stays only a couple of weeks, as soon as that one starts to work well with us he's gone and we have to start all over with a new one. The money they bring in is enormously helpful, though. None of them knows it, of course, but they could work for the same period of time just by writing to me."

On my way back to the seaside hovel where I'd rented a room for $1.50, the local pharmacist stopped me to say good night. His English, of which he was very proud, was reminiscent of *Beat the Clock*, the television game show in which a dozen words were randomly placed on a magnetic board, then a contestant would put them in sequence to form a sentence. He shook my hand vigorously as he smiled and said: "Sorry, we will be yesterday, no?"

We left early the next morning for the site a few miles south of Puerto López. The residents of Salango, accustomed to the comings and goings of the international expedition, waved hello as the jeeps rolled by. The dig itself adjoined a sardine-processing plant, the only other industry in the town of a couple hundred people. A wire fence surrounded five large holes, each about three to five feet deep. Trowels and sieves were handed out. Dirt from each hole, five to ten centimeters at a time, was dumped into a bucket, then shaken back and forth across a screen. Solid artifacts such as ceramic shards or pieces of pottery remained on top, while broken-up clods of dirt fell through the sieve. As each significant particle was uncovered, it was carefully labeled and cataloged with others found in the same spot. Sometimes an excavation team would be lucky enough to fit two newly found shards together. The previous day the crew had found a skeleton and remnants of a stone wall that dated back to the Valdivia period, 3000 to 1500 BC. Other discoveries came from the Manchalilla period, encompassing the next five centuries. Bowls, pots, and eating utensils gave some idea of how and what prehistoric Americans ate. The work went slowly, trowelful by trowelful, each successive pile of dirt representing another decade further back in time. When these piles become archaeological paydirt, they can yield finely sculpted impressions of animals and humans, some with musical instruments, showing domestic life among primitive Ecuadorans.

Figures of prehistoric *costeños* displayed at the Central Bank Museum in Manta had headdresses flaring up a foot and more from the forehead, as if wearing a vase fitted tightly to the skull. Could these have actually been the first hats woven from *toquilla* straw?

Whenever the crew at Salango made a genuine find, Clive, the British site photographer, came over to take a picture for the archives. "At another dig near here we used to have a little Ecuadoran boy," he said between shots. "He'd stand around and watch. Finally we hired him at a dollar fifty a day to carry things around. Then it was up to three dollars a day. He had more enthusiasm than anyone else on the team." Clive excused himself to go through some pottery shards. "I've got the world's best collection of photographs of the pigs here," he said upon his return. "They come up to the site to bathe in the sludge piles, they run alongside on every road, dogs chase them, they're in and out of every house, and they lounge in all the yards. There isn't much here that pigs aren't involved in. I've been watching them very closely. Do you suppose there's much of a market for a picture book on the pigs of Puerto López? I'd like to publish my collection."

Soon everyone retreated to the site headquarters, a large old building that housed the dig's findings and the crew's dog, Earthwatch. Upstairs, in the living quarters, I made a discovery of my own: a book called *Manabí*, by Marshall H. Saville, who wrote that *toquilla* fiber is so tough because it grows in coastal soil filled with salt and lime. "The most skillful Panama hat weavers," Saville reported, "receive seventy-five dollars gold for their efforts." The book was published in 1907.

The next morning I took the five o'clock bus back down the coast to Guayaquil, where I hoped to catch up with Domingo's straw from

Febres Cordero. The open-air wood-frame bus had five rows of closely spaced tiny benches. There was barely enough room between the benches for my legs to squeeze in. By synchronizing his route with low tide, the driver was able to use the hard-packed moist beach for a highway as we headed south. If he strayed too far to the left we'd get stuck in the looser, drier sand; too far to the right and we'd be swamped by the onrushing tide. As dawn broke we passed fishermen rowing their wooden crafts out to sea. A bracing mist slapped my face. I reached out my right hand and practically touched the Pacific Ocean. At that moment I wanted to ride that bus, uncomfortable as it was, forty-five hundred miles straight down the coast through Peru and Chile, and all the way to Tierra del Fuego.

CHAPTER ELEVEN

RED, WHITE, AND BLUE YELLOW FEVER

I arrived in Guayaquil and took a walk along the Guayas River. Ecuador is South America's westernmost country, and Guayaquil, due south of Miami, is its westernmost major port. Coastal traders always docked here, luring sailors, fortune seekers, pirates, and diplomats in their wake. In 1824, when Guayaquil was almost three centuries old, and a year after President James Monroe issued his doctrine warning European powers to stay out of the Americas, the State Department opened up a consulate here. It became the oldest continuously occupied United States post in South America.

William Wheelright, a New England sea captain in his twenties, filled the first consular spot. His tenure proved uneventful, but as a tireless promoter of steam-powered engines he greatly influenced nineteenth-century South America. When two of his steamships docked on the Chilean coast, the Valparaíso newspaper marveled at the "ponderous ships which moved without sail or oar." His Pacific Steam Navigation Company dominated coastal trade for decades. In 1850 he built South America's first railroad, a twenty-four-mile freight train through Chile's copper country.

United States representatives have always had strong feelings about Ecuador. The first United States chargé d'affaires in Quito, Delazon Smith, reported that he "witnessed little else than ignorance, indolence, wretchedness, dishonesty, and misery, on the part of the great mass of the people and selfishness, low cunning, sordid ambition, avarice, and blood-thirsty revenge on that of those who either lead or force the unconscious unthinking multitude. The country, too, is nearly as miserable as those who inhabit it. . . . They are so weak and defenseless, that three-thousand well-disciplined soldiers from the United States would march through their republic, conquering, taking and possessing every Town, City, and Province."

More agreeable was Matthew Palmer Game, who became consul in the 1850s when Panama hat exports reached unprecedented volume. An adventurer who had left his Philadelphia home at age seventeen, Game joined Simón Bolívar's revolutionary navy in Venezuela and eventually adopted Ecuador as his home. During his term, Nantucket whalers robbed Ecuador's prized Galápagos and their strategic importance was such that he suggested the United States annex the islands as a coaling station. Although nothing came of the idea, it became the first of many informal proposals between the two countries concerning ownership of the Archipiélago de Colón, as it is formally called. Most of Game's official time was spent dealing with troublesome sea captains, sailors, and traders from the United States. Descendants of his two Ecuadoran families—one legitimate, the other less so—form the Game Family Association, which each year still visits his grave on the Island of Puná in the Gulf of Guayaquil.

United States consular positions in Guayaquil, whether filled by career diplomats or merchants already living there, were less than enviable. Judging from their communiqués to Washington and elsewhere, they were subjected to filthy living conditions, painfully slow communications with the outside world, and a country whose government seemed to change with alarming alacrity. Yellow jack, as the dread yellow fever was known, was only one of many plagues that thrived. Ships carrying mail and supplies from abroad simply avoided Guayaquil during seasonal epidemics. On the political front, sometimes two or more military factions in different parts of the country claimed supremacy, and diplomats simply had to wait until the dust settled to determine with whom they should deal. Meanwhile, they spent an inordinate amount of time requesting the Stars and Stripes to wave above the consulate door on the Malecón.

- "I beg respectfully to inform the State Department that this consulate is in pressing need of a new large sized flag; the one sent last spring was so rotten that it was torn by the wind after a month's usage." Louis V. Prevost, November 1862.

- "[T]his city is, and has been for fifteen days past in a constant state of alarm and excitement. The revolutionists in this government . . . are organizing for an attack upon

Guayaquil. They have already taken possession of a small steamer . . . being owned by an American citizen carrying the American flag. . . . I consider it of absolute necessity that there should be a vessel of war in and about our Port for the protection of American property and interest." Prevost, to U.S. Navy Commander in Peru, August 1864.

· Flag request repeated, Prevost, February 1866.

· Flag request approved, June 1866.

· Another flag requested. Charles Weile, September 1872.

· Request made again. Weile, June 1873.

·· "The startling intelligence has just been received . . . of an attempt to assassinate President García Moreno. . . . The wounds inflicted are reported to be of a very serious nature and, it is feared, will prove fatal. . . . The political situation is grave and in the struggle for power . . . civil strife will be an inevitable result." Weile, August 1875.

· "This consulate has no large flag, the one now in use being old and worn out." Phanor M. Eder, April 1878.

· "[T]he salary is insufficient and the climate incompatible with good health. I have had the fever here twice . . . and my family have all been afflicted." Alexander McLean, May 1880.

· "My wife and four boys have suffered from the fever, and when scarcely more than convalescent one of my boys contracted small pox, and my wife fell victim to it nursing the boy." McLean, four months later.

· "I unfortunately met there the yellow fever . . ." Eder, in his second tenure, 1881.

· Ecuador exports 281,616 toquilla straw hats this year. Consular report, 1881.

· "Finding no one in Ecuador appearing to clearly hold the title of president or other title indicating Supreme head of the Government to whom I can present my credentials . . ." Martin Reinberg, explaining why he presented his diplomatic credentials to the local Collector of Customs, August 1883.

- "The flag . . . is getting ragged, and a new one should be sent—one sixteen feet in length." Horatio N. Beach, June 1885.

- "I have to state that the furniture . . . is old, worm eaten, and in a most delapidated and disreputable state." William B. Sorsby, July 1891.

- "For several weeks I have suffered from the effects of a fever and my physician now advises a change of climate." Sorsby, February 1893.

- "Lives and interests of American citizens endangered. Naval force absolutely required. Presidential elections fixed 28 to 31 May. Telegraph wires to Quito cut." Reinberg again, May 1895.

- "I have long since learned to be surprised at nothing either absurd or indecent the average Guayaquil paper publishes." Perry M. De Leon, August 1901.

- "I am anxious to leave Ecuador. I am very tired of this country and the people, and like and respect them less. . . . The natives, of whom I believe ninety-five percent are Indian or of mixed blood, are generally ignorant and too indolent to improve their condition. The so-called better class have as a rule become equally distasteful to me and, barring a few, I now have as little to do with them as possible in a social way." De Leon, three days later.

De Leon got his wish during the presidency of Theodore Roosevelt, who decided to fill the consular spot with Thomas Nast, the famed political cartoonist. Nast's crusade against corruption and his drawings of the Democratic donkey and the Republican elephant had established him in the forefront of modern political cartoonists. Aware that Nast, then sixty-two years old, had fallen on hard times, Roosevelt wrote, "It seems to me it is a national duty to do something for the gallant old fellow." His secretary of state contracted Nast about the post: "The President would like to put it at your disposition, but if you think it too far away and too little amusing to a man with the soul of an artist, please say so frankly. . . ." Nast accepted.

Soon he sent the secretary of state a sketch of himself, satchel and golf clubs in hand. "Say the word and I am off," read the caption. His farewell cartoon in the *New York Herald* showed him arriving on the equator as the volcano Cotopaxi erupts, alligators and dinosaurs prowl about, and, in the sweltering heat, the skull of death emerges from a box labeled YELLOW JACK.

Before Nast presented himself in July 1902, according to his biographer Albert Bigalow Paine, the local press had suggested that its readers rise up against the people sent by the United States. Nast won them over with a series of friendly cartoons run on the front page of *La Nación*, an afternoon daily. One showed him holding up the United States flag outside the consulate on October 9, Guayaquil's independence day, and shouting, "*Viva el Nueve de Octubre!*" Another mocked the coronation of King Edward VII of Great Britain. A third celebrated the first run of the railroad to the country's interior.

Nast wrote home to his wife of the conditions he saw around him. "Mice, rats, mosquitos, fleas, spiders and dirt all thrive. Water scarce," went one letter. "I hope I will live to die in some other place. Things are bad enough without my being buried here," another read. "The so-called 'best people' have made their exits on account of Yellow Fever. The steamers do not stop here. They go on south. That alarms the people here even more." Nast passed his time reading the Encyclopaedia Britannica and drawing. He looked out his door to see dogs "dirty, starved, wild." With his letters he sent sketches of street vendors selling Panama hats. As for the coffee, Nast proclaimed it "vile. The nearer one gets to the place it grows, the worse it is made." A week later, he added, "hot water is unknown here, except in coffee that is nearly all water." Another week passed: "Well, I had to get a coffee pot. Worse and worse. Could not stand it any longer. Alcohol lamp does the boiling."

In late November he complained, "my limbs get stiff and crampy." At the end of the month nausea set it. On December 7, 1902, less than five months after he arrived, yellow fever claimed the great political cartoonist thousands of miles from home. His effects included a painting of industrialist J. P. Morgan, an equestrian outfit, three Panama hats, and a revolver.

CHAPTER TWELVE

ALFARO LIVES

Thomas Nast's short tenure took place during the sweeping reforms of Eloy Alfaro's Liberal Revolution. Although temporarily out of office, the general from Montecristi greatly influenced the changes being wrought upon his country. His time was spent shuffling from Quito, where he had installed Leonidas Plaza Gutiérrez as president, to Guayaquil, his base of support, and Central America, where he still maintained business operations. He sent his son, Olmedo, to the U.S. Military Academy at West Point, but Cadet Private Alfaro dropped out after a year and set sail for Europe. In Guayaquil, Eloy often stayed at his married daughter's home in Las Peñas, a small neighborhood so close to the Guayas River that eddies lap up against the back wall of each house. Eloy Avilés Alfaro, grandson of the revolutionary hero, still lives in that same house on Numa Pompillo Llona Street.

The home of Eloy Alfaro's bachelor grandson is full of memories and mementos. Nearing seventy years old, he maintains the house much as it was when the general himself stayed there. He greeted me at the door in an undershirt. Tall, with a freckled bald head, Eloy seated me in a parlor twenty feet high, looking across the river. He recited family history at the drop of a hat.

"My grandfather was in love with a Panamanian woman, so he kept returning there to sell *sombreros de paja toquilla*, but also to see her. My mother lived in different countries in Central America, wherever the family happened to be living in exile. When he became president, my grandfather moved the whole family back here. The room we're sitting in now was the living room and the library. The dining room was downstairs and the servants lived in the attic. Now I rent out the top and bottom floors. We have a few things left that are of historic or intrinsic value, like photographs, but anything worth money has been stolen." *El nieto*, the grandson, pulled a military jacket and hat out of a closet. "All the silver has disappeared. Only the jacket remains. This furniture here"—he rapped on an old cabinet—"came from my grandfather. And up here"—he reached above the cabinet—"are his sword and his cane. The cane appears in all the formal photographs. Once when my grandfather repaid a loan made by another country, they sent him a kickback. It was traditional. He returned it, so they sent him this sterling silver tea set instead." He motioned me over to look at some elegant flatware designed with the country's coat of arms and his grandmother Ana's initials.

We talked more about his grandfather and the Liberal Revolution that transformed his homeland. "The Catholic Church said my grandfather was an atheist. At the time if you were not a Catholic you couldn't be a citizen. Period. But you can tell that an atheist would never act the way my grandfather did. He was simply against priests who used the Church to fight their own battles for their own convenience." General Alfaro was assassinated by a Papist mob after he had been arrested and sent to the main jail in Quito. "They got into the prison and dragged him through the streets. His body was tossed in an *hoguera bárbara*," a barbarous bonfire.

"My mother always used her father as an example. Hardly a day went by without mention of him around the house. On Good Friday he would always invite twelve poor people to dinner. My mother carried on that tradition. Because they were so poor and old, some were not very clean and we didn't want to serve them. But my mother said we have to thank God we can share our food. You must be humble and serve them, because one of these days the situation may be reversed. Now I carry on the same tradition."

This seemed an opportune time to present my cockamamy theory about Panama hats and the Liberal Revolution. I would never again get so close to the source. If *el nieto* supports it, I thought, I'll have made my contribution to Ecuador's history. If not, I'll discard it for good, as so many people had already counseled. "And so it seems clear to me," I said, leaning forward, "that Panama hats are responsible for the great Liberal Revolution that your illustrious grandfather led." (In Latin America, always speak in superlatives of successful revolutions and dead grandfathers.) "Right?"

Eloy Avilés Alfaro paused. I had diverted the flow of a conversation that he must have taken part in hundreds and hundreds of times over the years. "Well, yes," he finally said. "It's true he made a fortune selling Montecristi hats in Panama, and he did spend it all on the Revolution, financing ships and making other arrangements. So, yes"—he broke into an odd grin—"you are right. I've never thought of it that way."

El nieto poured some drinks. "In 1896 we had the big fire. This town used to be like a tinderbox for six months of the year, and every twenty or thirty years the whole place would burn down. After the fire of 1896, Guayaquil was rebuilt with the same architecture. At the time the buildings were very colonial, with stone streets in front. Wild vegetation used to grow right next to Las Peñas—medicinal plants and herbs, and quinine trees. One tubercular man improved himself so much with the herbs here that people started coming to him for help. He became a famous *curandero*," a healer, "and he set up beds to attend to the sick. People from town built houses here for the rainy season, when the yellow fever epidemics were most severe. It was cooler than in the middle of town."

Yellow fever, malaria, hookworm, dysentery, bubonic plague, typhoid fever, and other diseases visited Guayaquil regularly. A lack of gutters, sewers, pavement, and fresh water helped spread the sickness; many streets remained under a foot of green, slimy water half the year. Mosquito netting was mandatory. Rats ran through the best of homes with impunity, often carrying off lighted candles to munch on in their lairs. As construction progressed on the canal in Panama, the United States applied diplomatic and economic pressure upon Ecuador to force a sanitation campaign in Guayaquil. If you don't act now and do it our way, the veiled threat implied, transcanal ships will be quarantined from our port. General Alfaro called for cooperation with the United States effort, but not until a private medical team from the Rockefeller Foundation arrived was the volatile issue of having United States government doctors cleaning up an Ecuadoran city averted.

"When my older brother Colón was consul to San Francisco, I went there and took classes at Berkeley," Avilés continued. "I worked in a cannery for a couple of years. When I came back I went into the export-import business and worked for the Union Oil Company of

California. In World War II, I returned to the States to train as a pilot with the Army Air Force."

Sr. Avilés took off his bifocals and asked me to read a letter in English from a European researcher that had arrived the previous day. It had been addressed to "Grandson of Eloy Alfaro, Guayaquil, Ecuador." "You know, the Alfaro name doesn't belong to the family anymore. It belongs to the country. It's used by political parties, liquor stores, and schools. I supported the Radical Alfaro Front candidate in the last presidential election. I spoke at the opening of a housing cooperative bearing the family name, and I said if this project ends up corrupt like all the rest, I'll petition to have the name changed." A nascent guerrilla group believing that the goals of the Liberal Revolution have been betrayed by decades of oligarchies has also appropriated the family name: "*Alfaro Vive Carajo*," which loosely translates to "Alfaro lives, you sonuvabitch."

El nieto went to change into his evening clothes, leaving me to look out the window. A gentle breeze blew off the Guayas, and the sound of the river rubbing the lower wall cast a spell of serenity. "My mother said that she used to see pirate boats from that window," Avilés called out from the next room. "We used to see passenger ships and oil tankers on the river. Cargo ships would haul molasses from inland farmers. The river was about their only form of transportation. From the balcony there you can see swallows and flocks of little parrots. On clear afternoons Mount Chimborazo is visible for twenty minutes or so. The snow peaks have touches of red and yellow from the sun. During the rainy season we can see the shadows of the Andes."

My host emerged clean-shaven, wearing a newly pressed white shirt. For cuff links he used buttons from his grandfather's military uniform. "Follow me. I want to show you something." We went back into his bedroom, where a hammock extended from wall to wall, and he carefully pulled a plastic bag down from a shelf. "This is my Panama hat. It comes from the same town as my grandfather." I admired its laced crown and tight weave. "Yes, well, I haven't worn it in a while."

We set back down next to the parlor window. "On October ninth every year I invite some friends over to celebrate Guayaquil's independence. We dip a cup into the river and drink to the memory of my grandfather." I recalled what I had read about alligators in the Guayas

River from Edward Whymper, famous throughout Ecuador for having scaled its most difficult peaks in the 1890s, and from William E.
Curtis, in his turn-of-the-century account, Between the Andes and
the Ocean. Of alligators, Whymper wrote, "the natives do not seem
troubled by their proximity, though it is admitted they do occasionally
chew incautious children." Curtis had seen Guayaquileños, stark naked
except for yard-wide *toquilla* straw hats on their heads and long knives
between their teeth, hunt alligators for their hides in the Guayas. "They
swim along among the 'gators, and when one of the reptiles opens his
jaws and goes for him the swimmer dives, leaving his hat on the surface
for the alligator to chew on, and plunges the knife into the monster's
vitals." Avilés seemed amused by the descriptions but discounted any
current danger, either from alligators or their hunters. "We have a saying here: 'My hat instead of myself.'"

Avilés, like the other Guayaquileños I'd met, was annoyed by
Quito's attitude toward his city. "We've been abused by national governments. Eighty percent of the country's money is earned here, and
what do we get—maybe five percent of that. We should give the country twenty percent and keep eighty to better our city. People here are
disillusioned. No matter how hard we work, almost all of the money
goes to Quito. The *serranos* get mad at us. Well, I'm proud to be a *mono*.
All the oil money that the state petroleum monopoly makes ends up
in Swiss bank accounts. This is a marvelous country with a wonderful
climate. We have year-round fruit and vegetables. But the people are
no good. They want to get as much money out of you as they can."

Some forty homes line the one narrow street of Las Peñas. In many
ways it resembles the finer sections of Georgetown in Washington,
D.C., during quieter days. Plaques honor the four Ecuadoran presi-
dents who have lived there. Hidden away from the noise and traffic
that characterize the rest of the city, Las Peñas has retained its archi-
tectural integrity and dignity. "Folks here don't want this to become
a vulgarism with all that commercialization. I want some families to
live here like we had in the old days. Maybe we could have a couple
of small restaurants and art galleries and antique shops, but we don't
want to popularize the neighborhood so that it becomes a tourist place
for drinking and scandals." To this end Avilés heads the Committee
for the Preservation and Improvement of Las Peñas and Cerro Santa

Ana, the adjoining crowded lower-class neighborhood. "We are fighting to preserve the area. The rich own homes in Las Peñas, but many of them let their houses fall apart so they can turn the land into skyscrapers and make even more money. They should have some civic pride and help preserve it. If a man, rich or poor, smart or not, has no tradition, he has nothing. The only tradition the people here have is *¡chingo!*—the sound of money. When they hear that sound everybody looks. That's what they all want. That is their tradition."

The grandson continued. "There is a man down the street who wants to alter the façade of his building and turn an old apartment into a garage. That would mean more cars on the street, and that would be terrible. He said he had a permit from the city, but I checked, and he didn't. I filed a *denuncia* against him"—a sort of people's indictment—"and he got furious. He threatened to wreck my house and cut me up with a knife."

Avilés brought out a fancy glass jar half-filled with Eau de Cologne Jean Marie Farina, bottled by Rogers and Gallet. "My grandparents used this, and so did my parents. It smells clean and fresh at the same time." He pulled out a neatly folded handkerchief from the top drawer of a dark wooden dresser and dampened it with some of revolutionary General Eloy Alfaro's personal French cologne. With a regal flourish he presented it to me: "There. Now you are part of the Alfaro clan." As we walked out the door, he slipped a derringer into his pocket. "You can't tell anymore. This fellow did threaten me, and Cerro Santa Ana is a rough neighborhood." He tapped his pocket. "I carry it everywhere these days."

PART TWO

CHAPTER THIRTEEN

TO MARKET

The overstuffed sack holding Domingo's *toquilla* straw had arrived in Guayaquil before I did. A truck picked it up along with a dozen more from Febres Cordero and other small towns nearby, and carried it to Victor González's *bodega* near the corner of Colón and Pedro Moncayo. The storefront warehouse, which González shared with a middleman in the grain trade, was in the thick of a noisy neighborhood full of brawny men pushing heavy carts, noxious fumes, sweating laborers, barefoot Indians, busloads of new arrivals from the countryside, vendors hawking newspapers, rawboned women balancing platters of fruit on their heads, and the street-smart cries of abandoned children. Most intersections lacked sufficient traffic lights or stop signs; drivers played "chicken" every time one cleared. Pedestrians maneuvered among moving cars, outflanking a taxi here, a truck there. The few working lights gave rise to the definition of an Ecuadoran nanosecond: the length of time between the instant a light turns green and the first honk of a horn. González pointed to the straw from Febres Cordero. "That will go on a bus for Cuenca tomorrow," he yelled over the din. "I'll ride on the same bus if I can."

A couple of days later Victor González brought his bundles of *toquilla* straw into the ground floor of his house in Cuenca and stored them in a front room. Along with a handful of other intermediaries, González supplied the tens of thousands of weavers in Cuenca and the surrounding countryside with the raw material for their income. Distribution of straw from the coast depends upon availability, which in turn is determined by transportation, climate, work force, and price. Victor and the others had worked out a system, at once elaborate and simple, to get the *paja toquilla* to the weavers.

The main funnel, regardless of destination, is the weekly market, which virtually every weaver attends, selling hats woven the previous week and buying raw straw for the following week. The *feria de paja*, almost always held in conjunction with a larger market, is like an informal convention at which Indians, *campesinos*, *cholos* (non-Indian peasants), and others buy and sell food and supplies for the coming week. More important, the *feria* brings together for one crowded day every week small merchants, weavers, and farmers who raise livestock and grow crops on the arable part of their rocky land. News and rumors circulate from seller to buyer, merchant to consumer. An increasing number of women wear slacks, but most still cling to the traditional calf-length full skirt hemmed with colored embroidery. The skirts and the women who wear them are called *cholas*. Gangs of pickpockets are not uncommon at the main Cuenca market; usually one of three *cholas* working together will slit open the purse of a shopper and reach inside for money while the other two jostle and distract the unsuspecting victim.

Straw brought in from the coast gets trucked from Cuenca to Azogues, Sígsig, Biblián, and smaller towns. By the time it reaches the weekly market, the *toquilla* straw bundled in Febres Cordero and other villages on the coast has been graded in three basic quality levels and broken down into smaller quantities. Slightly fewer than three thousand *tallos*—shriveled-up palm fronds, each with a dozen or so strands attached to a common stem—make up one *bulto*. Victor González has paid a bit more than a penny and a half for each *tallo*, and sells them at close to two cents a *tallo*. His profit before expenses—a warehouse in Guayaquil, transportation for himself and his straw to Cuenca—comes to about thirteen dollars a *bulto*.

From the *campo* they come every Thursday morning with produce, children, and sometimes even livestock on their backs—Indians and *cholos*, trudging toward Cuenca. Out of the hills and valleys, emerging from folds in the Andean fields, they flag down buses and trucks headed for town. Most of them, even children, wear well-lacquered Panama hats.

The straw market in Cuenca can be deceptive at first. No more than seventy-five people appear at any one time, but the turnover is gradual and fluid, as women sitting on the ground behind small piles of straw bargain with weavers who come for their weekly supply. With the discriminating eye of a jeweler, each weaver peruses the straw in every saleswoman's pile, looking for coarseness, size, length, coloration, and blemishes. They gently tug at the ends testing for strength and suppleness, then arc a few strands to gauge their pliability. Knowing that from this purchase their income for the next few days will be determined, they fondle the *paja* with expertise, almost stroking it. (In fact, the phrase *hacerse la paja*, literally "to do the straw to one's self," means, in slang, to masturbate.)

A four-foot-tall *chola* with a plastic sack of eggs in her left hand and a basket of fruit on her back knelt barefoot in front of a pile of *paja* as if before an altar. At seven a.m. she was still early enough to select from the widest assortment of straw. After running her dirty hands along half the straw for sale, she bargained with one saleswoman for five *tallos*—enough straw to weave one coarse Panama hat. Unable to talk the lady down from two and a half cents a *tallo*, she reached in her purse for change. Her face remained expressionless throughout the transaction. A boy of six with the face of a grandfather had accompanied her, carrying her eggs for her as she departed.

Azogues, the capital of the Province of Cañar, lies a good forty-five minutes northeast of Cuenca. It is Ecuador's Podunk, the stereotypic town filled with dull-witted rubes. In this province, it is said, more alcohol is consumed than milk. On Saturday, people fill every street corner and crowd the municipal market. Trucks from the countryside continually load and unload their human cargo. An obscenely drunken *cholo* in a dark suit and felt hat staggered down the main street at a forty-five-degree angle to the ground, his right arm draped around his wife's neck as she lugged him forward one step at a time. His marinated eye glazed at the sky; the other eye socket was empty. Every ten feet he bounced off some storefront wall, giving new life to his lopsided gait. Passersby ignored the couple until the man collapsed completely. Then they helped his wife drag him away from the gutter and out of the flow of traffic. A few feet away a crowd gathered around a woman selling little *sucre*-sized tins of lip balm; she hawked it through a portable speaker as if it were the greatest salve since Simón Bolívar. Three men walked by hoisting a wooden Jesus on their shoulders. One held out a tin can to collect money from the faithful who approached to touch the crown of thorns, kiss the robe, and genuflect. Tacked to Jesus' robe was a police permit allowing the trio to solicit.

Dozens of barefoot women sat behind piles of straw, laughing at jokes told in a raspy, high-pitched Quichua cackle. The straw in Azogues cost between two and three and a half cents a *tallo*, the thinner and more uniform *paja* at the upper end of the scale. The women who sell straw to weavers, usually weavers themselves, earn about half a penny above cost for each *tallo*. On a good market day they might make a dollar or more. During the rest of the week they often sit in their doorways at home, weaving hats while waiting for others to come and buy straw they've laid out on the sidewalk before them. Weavers who get just five *tallos* for coarse hats often buy enough for three or more hats at a time. Ten and sometimes more *tallos* are needed for a more delicate weave. The *finos* from Montecristi require still more straw, and of a far superior quality.

The market at Biblián, another twenty minutes north, was much the same as that at Azogues, except on a smaller scale. The hat weaving here is of a generally better quality, and the straw, delivered by Victor González, is of a correspondingly better grade. Aside from straw, Biblianeros could buy the following at their weekly market: bananas, potatoes, plantains, beans, fruit, tomatoes, bread, corn, avocados, onions, garlic, carrots, sauces, baskets, pepper, lettuce, *choclos*, meat, flowers, cheese, rope, bandages, Alka-Seltzer, thread, knives, sunglasses, scissors, toothpaste, and Quaker Oats. At eight o'clock one Sunday morning traders at the local market were entertained by the Municipal Band: three clarinets, two trumpets, and three drums. The woodwind, brass, and percussion sections were each playing different tunes. A man wearing boots, his bottle of *aguardiente* falling from a pocket, delighted onlookers by dancing alongside the marching band. After a couple of minutes he found the beat, then he found a friend, and the two men danced off behind the musicians as they wandered down the dirt streets of Biblián.

Back at the marketplace, a six-man volleyball game paused between serves to let a *chola*, oblivious to the game, walk through center court with her emaciated dog. Less hurried than the crowds at Cuenca or Azogues, Biblianeros meandered through their primitive shopping center greeting friends from the smaller towns far from the main highway. From the eastern hillside the white Shrine of Our Lady of Rocío looks down into Biblián, a perpetual reminder to the townspeople of a drought in the late 1800s that ended the same day they all prayed extra hard to the Virgin Mary for rain. A visit to the shrine is worth "a hundred days indulgence to whomsoever visits the sanctuary," according to Victor von Hagen, "said indulgence to be applied to souls in Purgatory."

Among the hundreds of shoppers at Biblián's Sunday market, Isaura Calderón Encalada de Ojeda, fifty-one years old, bought food to feed herself and her family—seven in all, including her ninety-year-old mother and her four-year-old grandson. And she paid about twenty cents for enough straw to make a *sombrero de paja toquilla* woven *brisa* style, the most popular weave exported to the United States. That same month, a hat shop in San Diego, California, placed its order with Resistol and a few other companies for spring and summer hats, to be delivered half a year later. Among the selections were a few dozen genuine Ecuadoran-straw Panama hats, woven *brisa* style.

CHAPTER FOURTEEN

MUSCLING IN ON THE SOMBRERO TRADE

Neither Isaura Calderón de Ojeda nor Victor González nor any of the tens of thousands of others in the Cuenca area whose income at least partially derives from Panama hats would be in the business at all were it not for B. Ugalde and Bartolomé Serrano. *Toquilla* straw first appeared in Cuenca in 1835, but the art of hat weaving did not initially catch on. Few people there knew the craft, straw delivery from the coast was painfully slow and hopelessly erratic, and once the hats were completed, middlemen who took them by mule train to the coast for export were unreliable. Religion was the only thriving business in Cuenca and the surrounding towns, and the Roman Catholic hierarchy was very selective about whom it admitted into its fold. Most Indians and *mestizos* were tethered to the land and its owners. Indentured and miserably treated, they had little hope of escaping and less chance of an independent income.

Casting about for an industry to bring a trickle of cash flowing through the region, the Municipal Council of Cuenca unanimously passed an ordinance in 1844 establishing a school to teach *toquilla*-straw-hat weaving, which included a factory to process the woven hat bodies. The area lent itself to straw weaving: The air was drier than on the coast, where high humidity caused brittle straw; the temperature was cooler, which allowed more hours for weaving each day; and, most important, people willingly accepted lower wages. The city of Cuenca supplied the building, bought the straw, and hired the school's first director, B. Ugalde. He was paid a commission for every ten apprentices he enrolled plus half the profits from their hats. The students received the other half.

The next year Bartolomé Serrano brought in teachers from Jipijapa to teach hat weaving to the people of Azogues, where he was magistrate. In addition to offering classes in his domain, Serrano was authorized to "pursue and punish the vagabonds who did not want to look for work or learn to weave." As a result, twenty "important men" of Azogues were jailed and forced to learn hat weaving. Serrano gave the first crop of hats to the police, and the next to peasants—provided they agreed to learn hat weaving. "The finest hats," read one history, "were woven in Biblián and were very much liked in Cuenca and Guayaquil."

Serrano's efforts were rewarded with an assassination attempt. One day a stranger, Ponciano García, approached Serrano on the pretext of arresting him, then lunged at him with a knife. Serrano's bodyguard, the story goes, grabbed García's knife, whereupon the would-be assassin admitted that he had been sent from the coast with orders to murder Serrano for muscling in on the *sombrero* trade.

The demand for fine *toquilla* straw hats skyrocketed as the Isthmus of Panama became the distribution center into Central and North America. By 1850 weavers in the province of Azuay produced more than two thousand hats a year, a growing supply to meet a seemingly limitless demand. Already popular in the United States, the hats were taken to Paris for the 1855 World Exposition by a Frenchman living in Panama. The finest one was given to Napoleon III, who showed off his hat from Panama everywhere. The year that Ecuadoran revolutionary and hat exporter Eloy Alfaro turned twenty-one, half a million *sombreros de paja toquilla* were shipped from the Port of Guayaquil. In both North America and Europe they were universally known as Panama hats.

I came by much of this information from Dr. Ernesto Domínguez, a native of Azogues who works for the Cuenca Chamber of Commerce. A solemn man, his eyes lit up when he learned of my interest. "Wait here," he instructed, putting pressing business aside. "I found it," he said when he returned a few minutes later. He waved about a neatly handwritten sheet of paper on which he kept statistics going back year by year into the nineteenth century detailing how many hats had been exported and to which countries. More than five million straw hats were exported from Cuenca in 1977, the peak year since records were first kept. "We measure everything in dollars because that's how the export houses are paid regardless of country. That's the main reason business has slipped in recent years—the currencies in Brazil and Mexico have devalued so much that dollars are much harder to come by in both countries. Together, they accounted for a big part of our business."

CHAPTER FIFTEEN

HENRY MILLER'S NEPHEW

The dollar is the imperial currency, not just in international trade but in the smallest *víveres* outlet as well. No matter how well acquainted you are with a Latin American town and make friends with its people, you still symbolize the gringo dollar. No one hesitates to ask about the United States. Everyone wants to know: What is your income? How much does a watch cost? A television? A car? A house? A hat? A plane ticket between the United States and Ecuador? During that pause suspended between the question and the answer the inquisitive *mestizo* comes one tiny step closer to that material world. He imagines himself, for a moment, directly in touch with the dollar and all that it represents.

"What is it like to teach in the United States? Do you think we could get jobs there?" These questions came from students at the Universidad Estatal de Cuenca, whose class in Culture and Civilization of the English-Speaking Countries I visited once more. The previous day classes had again been suspended for a political rally, virtually guaranteeing a day free of disruption. On my way over I had stopped to browse in a bookstore, struck by the wide range of books from Argentina, Mexico, and Spain. The few domestic offerings included *The Responsibility of the United States Government in the Territorial Mutilation of Ecuador*, published by the University of Guayaquil.

Most of the students aspired to teach English, the imperial language. They had just finished discussing the relationship between Herman Melville and Nathaniel Hawthorne, and they asked about contemporary United States authors. "Do you know Norman Mailer?" My last name was close enough for them. They were especially interested in Saul Bellow. "Do you like John Steinbeck?" They were familiar with *The Grapes of Wrath*, often compared to their own novel

Huasipungo, by Jorge Icaza, about the horrific treatment of Indian chattel in the Ecuadoran highlands. "Are any of our authors well known in America?" I counted on the fingers of one hand the Ecuadoran writers whose works had been translated into English. They felt better when I described the upsurge in interest in Latin American literature brought about, in part, by Gabriel García Márquez winning the Nobel Prize for Literature. Imagine, a South American writer—a neighbor, no less, who writes about life along the Pacific Coast!—recognized with the world's foremost literary honor.

"Well, we want to know about the decline of American morals. Is it true?" "Is *what* true?" I replied. "You know, that you have no values left in the States." Shot. Kaput. Bankrupt. Another grand experiment down the drain. My answer, an awkward and uncustomary defense of the United States, was overrun with further questions. "We have heard of the environmentalist movement. How big is it?" "We've been reading about Indians in U.S. history. Are they well treated now, or is it like our Indians here?" "What difference have you noticed between family life in America and in Ecuador?" "Are Eastern religions very influential?" "Why do you have so many vegetarians?" "What happens to the Mexicans and others who get caught coming into the United States illegally? For the ones who don't get caught, what sort of jobs can they expect?" "Do you think John F. Kennedy's brother will run for president?" "What do Americans think of our president?" I fudged that one; in truth, of course, only a handful of people north of the Panama Canal can locate Ecuador, much less identify its president.

They were keenly interested in United States domestic politics. "You have a two-party system in a country of two hundred million. Do you have any minor parties? We never hear about them. Here we have fewer than ten million people but we have seventeen political parties." "What is the difference between the Republican Party and the Democratic Party? From here they look so similar." They don't look a whole lot different close up, I confessed.

La Fuerza del Cariño (*Terms of Endearment*) had just opened at a local theater. "Is America really like that?" "Well, parts of it are, yes," I said, warming to my advisory role. "Actually that'd be a good movie to see. It shows some subtleties of American culture you don't find in many films here." "Oh, we know all about American culture," a student replied. "Yes," another followed, "we watch *Dallas* all the time!" "*Dynasty* too," another chimed in. "We learn about your culture that way."

The next afternoon I was invited to sit in as three professors grilled an English major on her senior thesis—"Thomas Hardy: Harbinger of the Screenplay." She planned to leave Cuenca the following fall to attend an exclusive New England college to complete her education. Her family threw a graduation party for her that night. Fellow students mingled with faculty, relatives, and family friends. Servants brought out terrific food, and we toasted her success with Chilean wine. The elite of Cuenca gathered once again to celebrate another passage into their ranks.

"Excuse me," a man said as he introduced himself. "But are you related to Glenn Miller?" Older Ecuadorans remember the band leader from a visit to Salinas on the coast, where he entertained United States troops during World War II. Not in the slightest disappointed that Glenn and I were not related, he returned five minutes later, smiling. "Ah, I know. You are related to Henry Miller, the author. I just heard it."

Since my earlier visit to the university campus, a rumor had circulated that I was Henry Miller's nephew, in Cuenca to conduct interviews. The few times I was confronted with the story I denied it, which of course gave it more credibility. Now it seemed that half the faculty at one of the country's most prestigious universities was convinced— nay, honored—that the nephew of the well-known American writer had graced their campus. I was, after all, of the same name and profession, and I was writing about life halfway between the Tropic of Cancer and the Tropic of Capricorn. Did they need further evidence? Nothing I could say would dissuade them.

"Well?"

Chitchat around my corner of the room suddenly ceased as the guests awaited my reply. Being Henry Miller's nephew wouldn't be such a bad gig for a while, I thought to myself. Surely no one here knows anything about his real nephews, if indeed he had any. If I play my cards right, I could probably dine out on Uncle Henry for months. First I'd spend a few weeks in Cuenca perfecting my ruse, then take my show on the road all over the continent—Lima! La Paz! Buenos Aires! Rio! Caracas! Bogotá! I'd stay one step ahead of the U.S. Information

Agency, which would put its junior-most officers on my trail. What finally convinced me to forgo my celebrity status—all in the space of five seconds—was not so much conscience as caution. I had only a passing familiarity with Henry Miller and his works. I hated to disappoint them.

CHAPTER SIXTEEN

BIBLIÁN WEAVERS

The seventy-five minute bus ride to Biblián the next morning was smooth enough to sleep through. By now I knew not to react to sudden stops, frequent swerves, or excess commotion. Biblián, whose Sunday market I had visited, attracted me because it was far enough out in the countryside to avoid the excesses of Cuenca but close enough to reach with no trouble. Its residents, fewer than fifteen thousand, led conventional small-town lives with marginal incomes, substandard health, and limited literacy. Walking all its streets took less than an hour. Friendly faces invited me into their one-room homes for low talk and instant coffee. Often I'd be seated in the one chair, shaky, next to the one table, wobbly. In many houses a burlap curtain draped over a series of interlocking coat hangers separated the kitchen from the bedroom. "You see that house across the street?" one woman asked, pointing up the hill. "The best *toquilla* hat weaver in town lives there. He's home now. Why don't you visit him?"

César Vicuña sat upstairs in his two-story house whose walls were made of mud mixed with hay. The first floor was alive with cats and piglets playing in the middle. An empty light socket hung from a frayed wire overhead. A series of unstable planks formed the steps that reached a hole in the corner of the second floor. Flush against one wall was a double bed covered with a tattered bedspread. A smaller bed leaned against an adjoining wall. An outdated calendar tacked above it partly covered a faded image of Jesus. Next to it were two small mirrors and a poster of multiplication tables for the four children who lived there. A cardboard box in the corner served as a clothes closet. A hot-water bottle and a small can of 3-in-One oil rested alone on a shelf. Sunlight streamed in through the two open-air windows surrounding the one piece of furniture, a chair in the middle of the floor on which sat the master weaver of Biblián.

Señor Vicuña wore a wool poncho over some well-worn pants, a Panama hat, and old sneakers. He sat hunched over. A flat board supporting a wooden hat block rested on his lap. Few people express interest in his hat weaving anymore, he said. "I've been doing it all my life. No one else in town makes *finos* like this anymore." The hat in his lap, about half finished, looked like creamy-white linen. Hundreds of needle-thin fibers hung from the edge. Vicuña talked as he wove, his eyes sharply focused on the fibers his hands continuously maneuvered over, under, and around each other. "The first six inches of this hat took me fifteen days to complete. That's the hardest and most import-ant part. The rest of the crown took three weeks. From there it takes three more weeks to finish." His fingernails were as thin as a knife as he split a thin fiber still thinner to lay into place on his masterpiece. "I made three hats for Velasco Ibarra while he was president." He took a cornless cob out of a small bowl of water and combed the loose straws with it. "One of them cost three thousand *sucres*," more than $750 at the time. The hat he worked on as we spoke, as fine as any to come from Montecristi, would bring him more than $50, he estimated. "I'm seventy-one years old now. I don't wear glasses. I need them, but I can't afford them."

He paused in his labor and carefully took his work in progress off the block. The strands were so thin that when he held it upright it looked like a blond wig. "Not one drop of water can pass through this hat," he boasted. He turned the hat upside down, clutching it by its loose hairs, and poured a small bowl of water into it. "See?"

Before leaving I asked where I might find the *excusado*. "Bathroom?" Both César and his wife laughed. "We barely have a roof over our heads." Boards, tile, plastic, and planks lay scattered over decaying crossbeams above us. The sky shone clearly through the roof.

Back down the hill, on the other side of the Pan American Highway, Isaura Calderón de Ojeda sat in her little grocery store wait-ing for customers. The store, Mini Mercado El Rocío, caters to neigh-bors who need an item or two to tide them over until the following Sunday's market. Whenever three families live near each other any-where in the country, no matter how desolate the setting, it seems one of them assumes the role of grocer. When more than five families find themselves living close together, a second *tienda* opens up, competing with the first to see which can charge higher prices. The entire stock in Mini Mercado El Rocío consisted of two dozen different items.

While she waited, Señora Calderón wove her first hat of the week. Her mother, Catalina, who wove her first Panama hat during Eloy Alfaro's Liberal Revolution, sat nearby doing likewise. Once she could turn out six or more hats a week, but age had slowed her down to two, and sometimes one. Thirteen-year-old Janet, on the basketball team at the local Colegio Femenino, found time to weave a few every week. Her sister Eulalia, almost twice Janet's age, hadn't made a hat in a long while. She worked as a social worker when the government could afford to pay her, going through the countryside informing *campesinos* about nutrition and birth control. María Elena, three years younger, still made hats when she wasn't caring for her four-year-old son, Dany ("like Daniel Boone!"). Eighteen-year-old Carlota Beatríz blushed when I asked if she made hats. "She just got back from her honeymoon," her mom said laughing, as she slapped her daughter on the fanny, "and she doesn't spend her evenings weaving anymore."

Isaura's husband completed the eight-member household. He drove a small passenger van on a regular route between Azogues and Cuenca every day. A ceramic Jesus stood on its dashboard; a sticker advertising a travel agency in Hyde Park, New York, was plastered to its window. His garage next to the store was empty save for a bicycle hanging upside down. "Almost all of the weavers are women," María Elena said. "At least around Biblián. The men can make more money doing other things."

I was impressed with the intelligence and industry shown by Isaura and her family. I dropped by their place often to chat—something they invariably had time for—and both they and I grew to welcome the visits as they passed the hours weaving their Panamas. On Sundays they brought their finished hats a few blocks away to Adriano González, a *comisionista* who purchased all the hats produced in the Cantón of Biblián and sold them to the hat factories in Cuenca. Hundreds and hundreds of weavers line up at González's place Sunday mornings to trade in their artisan labor for money to buy food during the following week. "The real poor people," Isaura explained, "they sell their hats to

Señor González on weekdays so they can buy rice." Five minutes later an example walked through the door. She paid a few *sucres* for just enough rice to fill a small crumpled paper bag.

CHAPTER SEVENTEEN

INCAS AND INDIANS

Instead of visiting the Ojedas the next day, I went north, where the Cañari and other Indians lived. The Indians of the Andes—does there exist a worse-treated, more downtrodden slice of humanity? Subjected to whimsical rule, living in decrepit huts, horrendously overworked and miserably underpaid, they have been bypassed, for the most part, by recent advances in agriculture, commerce, and civil rights. Over the course of five centuries, the highland Indians have had to contend with Inca masters, Spanish subjugation, Catholic dominance, and, since national independence, exploitative local, provincial, and central governments. From each of these they have benefited only marginally and suffered greatly. The fertile *hacienda* land they have farmed has enriched its owners; the rocky plots they live on have kept them in poverty. Laws allowing them a measure of independence were barely worth the parchment they were written on. Priestly calls for brotherly love fell on deaf ears, even within the clergy.

Indians were "reduced to the most abject state of servitude and bondage," observed the Frenchman Laurent Saint-Criq when he traveled through the Andes in the 1870s. "These unfortunate beings, robbed of their country, are merely allowed to exist in it. . . . [T]he plunderers would only possess a barren waste without their labour." Saint-Criq's conclusion about the Indians and the land they work could be drawn in the twentieth century as well. They are, he wrote, "the degraded original proprietors, on whom the curse of conquest has fallen with all its concomitant hardships and penury."

Ecuador abolished slavery thirteen years before the United States did, but the act effectively freed only the fewer than twenty-five hundred blacks. For Indians, other forms of enforced labor continued. Contract servitude, called *concertaje*, was only a small step better than *huasipungaje*, a system that strangled them in a choke hold of perpetual debt. The practice required peasants to give a fixed amount of labor to a *hacienda* in exchange for a plot of land on which to farm and to live. The soil on the little plot was often impossible to till, the home too ramshackle to last beyond a few seasons, and the debt to the *hacienda* owner inherited by the worker's children after his death. When *hacienda* land was sold, title to the Indians went with it. With the notable exception of some enlightened landowners over the years, Indians, subjected to the *hacienda* manager and his underlings, were forced to pay tribute to the parish priest, endure beatings, and maintain a life of unrelenting hardship. They lay at the very bottom of a caste system so pervasive as to be invisible. Throughout its history Ecuador has adhered to this system religiously.

Efforts to abolish the more notorious forms of servitude have surfaced spasmodically in the national legislature, but not until 1964, under military rule, did change take place. The Law of Agrarian Reform came about mainly because domestic politics dictated it, but also as a result of pressure from the Alliance for Progress, the Kennedy-Johnson administration's effort to strengthen Latin American countries sympathetic to the United States. The act abolished the practice of exchanging land for labor and set a minimum wage for male farm workers in the *sierra* of forty cents daily.

Land redistribution was slow and haphazard. Peons who had never owned land before lacked the know-how to raise crops and livestock for market. Many were awarded land too poor for cultivation and too far from transportation to succeed. Some landowners avoided losing property by dividing their *haciendas* into smaller parcels and giving title to each of their children. Tens of thousands of *campesinos* still await land claims from an inefficient and often unsympathetic government agency. Even a generation past the abolition of servitude, teenage children of formerly indentured peons still carry on the servile traditions of their ancestors, lightly kissing the hand of the landowners who hire them. "*Sí, patroncito.*" Yes, dear master.

The plight of Indians in the *sierra* became more than recent history as I rode an hour north of Biblián to Ingapirca, a series of stone walls dating back to the latter half of the fifteenth century. The closer I got to Tambo, the turnoff for the Inca ruin, the more the mountains spread their folds, out of which trickled streams of water and Indians. Sunlight landed only in the valleys below. A tractor-trailer had recently jackknifed off the side of the road; cars, cattle, and *campesinos* had to detour through a gully. A crowd of Indians watched as a mammoth tow truck pulled the injured semi from the ditch where it had landed. The Indians, both male and female, wore longer and longer hair the farther into the province of Cañar I traveled. Most walked slowly but steadily on sturdy legs whose feet only occasionally wore shoes.

Hunched over, weather-beaten, and ageless, the Andean Indians seemed to be forever walking with heavy loads strapped to their backs. During the course of one week I saw them saddled with clothing, chickens, pigs, cattle (alive and butchered), babies, grandparents, firewood, straw, produce, cases of soft drinks, footlockers, milk jugs, furniture, bicycles, lumber, cinder blocks, sugarcane, pots of water, bundled newspapers, potatoes, tools, and tires. At the end of the nineteenth century, a historian wrote, a Cuenca aristocrat "had a grand piano imported from France carried on the backs of Indians over the Molleturu pass from the port of Guayaquil," and in this century "the first car in Cuenca was carried in on the backs of Indians." From the waist up they stoop over at a three-quarter angle to the ground, always looking as if they are headed into a stiff wind. Even when they are walking downhill they tread as if pulling themselves uphill. At times it seems as if the Indians carry the Andes themselves on their backs.

At Tambo the route to Ingapirca turns right. Along the dirt road covering the last few miles to the site, dozens of Indian construction workers in ponchos formed a seemingly endless brigade, passing huge rocks up a hill whose crest was barely visible. Finally Ingapirca came into view. It is of genuine Incan construction and architecture—trapezoidal stone blocks niched together, crafted with such precision that only a razor-thin mortar binds them. For generations Ingapirca's finely cut stone has supplied neighbors with home-construction material. Only portions of the ruin have been uncovered, and just recently has the government acted to preserve, protect, and explore it further.

The ruin includes the stone frame of a castle of sorts, whose front yard consists of a nine-level terrace. Other structures were probably rooms for storage and sleeping, plus what appears to be a seat or perhaps a small bath. A circle of rocks covers a tomb, according to legend. Damp and chilly winds swept across the plateau. The Inca Highway itself winds by the site, and I took great satisfaction in walking one mile of what was left of the 3,250-mile Highway of the Sun, upon which Tupac Yupanqui, Huayna Cápac, Atahualpa, and other Incas had traveled five centuries earlier. The path's most important point lies more than a thousand miles south at Cuzco, Peru, and according to Hernando de Soto was once wide enough "for six of my men mounted on horseback to ride abreast." A child of eight who lived nearby approached and without prompting sputtered out a two-minute recitation of the area's history.

Within sight of the ruins, farmers tilled a steep field with their oxen while others planted seeds in their wake. At twelve noon a bell rang out, and the *campesinos* dropped to the ground, unwrapped the scarves from their faces, and pulled out their lunch. The tightly terraced mountainside looked like aisles in an amphitheater. Children who lived in farmhouses along the Inca Highway skipped by after school, entertaining themselves with pebbles substituting for marbles, hopscotch, and, using a cardboard box for a ball, soccer. Ingapirca's groundskeeper, the one on-site employee, approached as I started up one walkway connecting several of the structures. "Take the other path if you can," he advised. "This one is older, and we're trying to preserve it as much as possible." He was excited because some archaeologists from Spain were due in a couple of weeks to renew excavation efforts. "Who knows what they will find?" the groundskeeper said. "So many things here are yet to be discovered."

A guide from the government tourism office pointed out various nearby rocks, one of which takes the shape of an armchair, another a turtle, a third appears as a monkey, and yet another as the face of an Inca. "Do you see them?" she asked brightly, motioning me to the spot from which they appear most visible.

I hesitated. "Not quite."

"Walk over here," she suggested. I moved a few steps closer and looked again. "Ah, yes. Of course," I said with a smile. "There's the turtle, that one's the monkey, the armchair is up there, and the Inca face is over there." She lit up too, pleased that I'd seen the images. In truth, I hadn't seen them at all, not a one, but by this time I'd learned the

Ecuadoran custom of politely feigning agreement regardless of the circumstances.

No one really knows what Ingapirca is all about, which makes it so tantalizing to archaeologists and tourism promoters alike. At the least it was a *tambo*, a resting spot along the Inca Highway at which the chieftans and their subordinates could spend the night. One theory speculates that Ingapirca was a depot for grain, another that it was a religious monument. A third theory, both elaborate and reasonable, suggests that Ingapirca was a lunar sanctuary.

A few days after visiting Ingapirca I returned to Biblián and dropped in at Mini Mercado El Rocío. Everything was going well; Isaura was finishing up her second hat of the week and had already paid forty-five cents for the straw to make a couple more. Three customers bought items totaling seventy cents during my brief visit.

To return to Cuenca I stood on the side of the road just south of town hoping to flag down a truck or a bus. An informal volleyball game was in progress between two *policías rurales*, across from whose station house I waited. With no words exchanged, they started hitting the ball to me, and I slapped it back. We continued for a few minutes, when one of the uniformed officers stepped out into the road to stop an old pickup truck and ask the driver for his papers. The man, who bore an uncanny resemblance to Moe of The Three Stooges, took out his registration. Although I was out of earshot, their gesticulations told the story. The driver asked why he had been stopped—he had done nothing wrong, his documents were in order, and he was in a hurry to get going. The cop listened patiently, nodded, then shook his head and finally took the driver by the arm. His partner joined him, and they escorted the hapless man across the street into their office. His wife watched from the pickup's front seat with helpless contempt; their children looked on from its bed.

A few minutes later the three emerged from the policemen's shack. One of the cops was pocketing some bills while the driver, continuing his protests, walked back to his truck. Our volleyball game resumed as the pickup pulled away.

When I returned to Cuenca to check out of my hotel, I ran into a situation I should have anticipated. I had stayed there on the recommendation of a government official in Quito who had assured me that arrangements would be made for my lodging to be *gratis*, or at the least the manager would grant—I think these were his exact words—"*un descuento sustantial*," a substantial discount. Even though it was written in the 1860s, Frederick Hasaurek's account in *Four Years Among the Ecuadorians* suggested this would happen: "This custom of making high sounding promises, which are not intended to be kept, is universal among Ecuadorians of the Sierra." James Orton, who passed through ten years later, agreed: "A newly arrived foreigner is covered with promises: houses, horses, servants, yea, every thing is at his disposal." Clearly a promise of hospitality was part of the national patrimony.

The hotel manager had gone fishing, and the desk clerk, who doubled as the bellman, knew nothing of any arrangement. Neither, it developed upon his return, did the manager. Orton, again: "But alas! The traveler soon finds that this ceremony of words does not extend to deeds. He is never expected to call for the services so pompously proffered." That was my mistake—calling for services so pompously proffered. When I was next in Quito, I made a point of visiting the pompous profferer. The hotel was satisfactory, I reported, but there was some mix-up with the bill. "Well, yes," he offered gamely. "There did seem to be some confusion, didn't there." And that was that.

CHAPTER EIGHTEEN

"ALL WE HAVE IS OURSELVES AND OUR STRAW"

After I had found another hotel, Adriano González picked me up in his Travelall for the ride once more to Biblián. The fifty-five-year-old *comisionista* was going to show me the most critical transaction the *sombrero de paja toquilla* goes through: the sale from the weavers scattered throughout the countryside to the exporting factories, via the middlemen.

Born and raised in Biblián, González moved to Cuenca when he turned twenty-five. He spends four days a week in Biblián; the rest of the time he delivers hats to the factories and handles the money end of his trade. At a height surpassing six feet, González towers above the hundreds of weavers he deals with every week. That morning he wore a shirt with snaps up the front beneath a cardigan sweater and a gray jacket. A woman sat in the backseat the entire trip as if she wasn't there; she didn't say a word, nor was she spoken to. For more than an hour the *chola* received less attention than a Latin American seatbelt. Even in the rearview mirror González didn't notice her. When the three of us got out in Biblián, she started carrying things into Adriano's house. I motioned to her, mouthing silently: "Who's that?"

"Oh, her." González seemed surprised that she had been acknowledged. "That's my servant," he said, at once answering the question and dismissing the subject.

"What's your name?" I asked her later.

"I'm the servant," she replied.

I introduced myself. "And you are—" I said, hanging the sentence in midair.

"—*para servirle*," she answered. At your service. In the highlands of Ecuador, it had become increasingly apparent, you either have servants or you are one. There's very little in between.

A long hallway led from Adriano's front door to a kitchen. A dark living room, also serving as the office, was off to the side. The main area, between the dark room and the kitchen, consisted of a large open space separated from the entranceway by a couple of low tables. An adjoining driveway had room for the Travelall, stacks of hats, and a dog. Inside plumbing distinguished the house from most Biblián homes. By the time we had parked the car and sat down in the open area, the servant already had water boiling for coffee and was heating up some bread she had bought at a storefront bakery down the block.

A light drizzle began. Across the street, Humberto, who sat on the ground in front of his house selling *tallos* of *toquilla* straw, started gathering up his *paja* to save it from the rain. Isabel, a neighbor from one block over, stopped him to pick out twenty-six *tallos*, enough to weave three or four hats. She gave him sixty-five cents, twenty-five cents less than he asked for. "I'll pay you the rest on Sunday when I get the money," she said, pointing her head toward González's place.

"You know," González said, "my work is very hard and I've become quite good at it. The main thing is that you have to keep up with it every month, every week, every day. I've known most of the weavers since they were little children. I know which ones will bring me the hats I ask for and which ones are not consistent. And I can tell which of the children will be good weavers when they get older. I encourage them. That's my greatest joy." I told him how the Ojeda family had impressed me. "Yes, and they're also reliable. That's the most important thing." We sat down for some bread and cheese and coffee.

"The weavers, they come in either before or after church on Sundays. Then they go to the market to buy their necessities and straw for next week. Some people avoid the crowd and bring their hats by during the week." The sound of the front door opening echoed from down at the end of the hall.

"My success has enabled me to have homes here in Biblián where I own eight houses, in Cuenca where I have four, and in Quito where I also have a house. I wish I had time today to take you out to my land. I have a cattle and apple farm near here." He called for the servant to bring me an apple, and waited until I had taken a bite. "Isn't it good?"

A barefoot woman entered with her young daughter, tracking in mud the same color as her skin. A triangular plastic bag shaped like a dunce cap covered her own well-worn *toquilla* straw hat to protect it from the rain. She pulled a Panama from another plastic bag and clutched it by its loose ends. She and her daughter stood waiting on one side of the table while we sat talking on the other side. Motionless, silent, invisible, she was willing to wait as long as necessary. Adriano walked over presently and took the hat from her. He pulled a short ruler out of his pocket and pressed it for a few seconds against the brim so that one end touched the crown and the other overlapped the edge. Next he pressed it against the length of the crown, and finally he laid it across the top of the hat measuring its diameter.

"Fifty cents," he said. His offer was more of a statement. The little girl looked up at her mother and the mother looked over at González. Timidly, she said, "I thought that you—"

"You should get sixty cents for a hat like this," González interrupted, "but it isn't wide enough. Look." He fetched the model hat he had shown her and the other weavers the week before and got out the ruler once more. "See the difference?" he spoke in a tone that was neither threatening nor upsetting, but rather as parent to child or teacher to pupil. "Next week if you bring in a hat with the right dimensions you'll get the full amount." She nodded and held out her hand. The *comisionista* pulled a roll of bills from his pocket and peeled off fifty cents in *sucres*; to the daughter he gave a couple of *sucre* coins, a smile, and a pat on the head. The mother nodded, mumbled something unintelligible, turned around, and walked out with her little girl. González tossed the hat in the corner.

Juan Peñafiel Verdugo walked in. He works exclusively for González, one of ten men who comb the countryside buying hats door to door. Everyone calls these men *perros*, dogs, snarling through the *campo* fetching hats and bringing them to their master. The term is no compliment, but it's been in use for so long it has lost most of its bite. Peñafiel carried with him twenty-eight high-quality hats from Barrio Nuevo in Guapán, a small town to the east, where he spends Wednesdays and Fridays calling on the same weavers week after week. Adriano counted out the hats, piled them next to the barefoot lady's handicraft in the corner, and went into the office to enter Juan's count into his logbook and advance him some cash for the following week.

Perros also stand on street corners on market days, intercepting weavers on their way to the *comisionistas*. They pay slightly less than the *comisionistas*, but by selling to *perros* the weavers avoid the long lines and the trouble of going to González and the others. *Perros* anchor themselves to the same corner on the same day every week, often buying from the same women week after week.

"If you want to see a smaller town back in the *campo* where they make *toquilla* hats," Juan said, "come out to Guapán with me or go to Paute or Déleg." I had heard of Déleg; most of its male population was said to be living in the United States. "It's not just Déleg," he continued. "Everyone around here knows someone who has gone there. But they say Déleg sends the most."

I dropped in on the Ojedas that afternoon. They entertained me for an hour or so, and their almost ritualistic weaving of the hats grew more and more fascinating. Their craft, so skillful yet so mechanical, was the constant in their lives. The pride of the artisan, however, hardly ever burst through. Undervalued in its own country, the Panama hat must travel to foreign climes to be fully appreciated. María Elena wove as she kept one eye on Dany, each fiber placed in sequence at an angle over—or was it under?—the previous one. Her mother, Isaura, paused between weaving the crown and the brim on hers to rearrange items in the window of their store. Grandmother Catalina listened to the conversation, nodded, smiled, chatted in Spanish I couldn't understand, all the while moving straws between the forefinger and thumb on each hand. If each strand of *paja toquilla* had been a musical instrument, the Ojeda family store would have swelled with a symphony.

"Is there a saint or a special mass or a *fiesta* to honor the hat weavers or the straw?" I asked.

"¡No! ¡No hay nada!" There's nothing! they responded, practically in unison. But every job and crop is honored in some ceremony, I countered. You mean there's no celebration connected with the *sombrero de paja toquilla*?

"Well, we don't have anything to celebrate, really. The others have their unions with power. What do we have? Nothing. Just ourselves and our straw."

How many heads have been covered by Catalina's hats since she first started weaving Panamas? Figure an average of four hats a week from ages eight to sixty, three weekly for the next twenty years, and one a week to the present. Strip away an arbitrary amount for distractions and disabling illnesses, and round off to the nearest hundred hats. In all, since turning eight years old in 1903, Catalina Encalada Martínez de Calderón has woven fourteen thousand Panama hats.

"May I try it?" I blurted out. I don't know what possessed me to ask, but my question provoked great laughter. "No, really," I protested. "I mean it." They all looked at each other and smiled. "Sure," the *señora* said. "Sit here." I took her place on a low stool. Janet handed me eight *toquilla* fibers, all newly moistened from a corn cob kept in a small tin bowl of water. The family gathered in a semicircle to watch the foreigner's first attempt at what comes second nature to them.

"Put them in twos so they cross over each other," Isaura instructed. I put one pair of fibers in one direction, another flat on top at a ninety-degree angle to the first, and a third set in the direction of the first. As I started to put the fourth set down the first one came loose, which weakened the next two sets. I was back at the beginning.

The girls tittered at my effort. "I'm left-handed," I explained. "You know, *el diablo*," the devil. "It might come out all backwards. Maybe that's why it fell apart." Isaura took my hands as if they were extensions of her own and arranged the eight fibers in position. "Next you pull the short ends up. That becomes the very center of the crown. It's called *la rosita*." The *señora* completed the *rosita* for me and handed it back.

I was much less enthusiastic about continuing. "*Siga no más*," they insisted. Keep going. "Next, put the straw on the left down under while you hold the upper one." "Good." "One down, one over. The top left straw goes straight down to the bottom, and the next one on the left goes two under." "That's right—one up, one down." "Ah-ah—keep the cross-strands in place." Their instructions jumbled in my ears, yet for a few straws' worth of weaving I could see minuscule progress. "Pull on the edges to tighten it up a little."

But with each new cross-strand I added to the outer edge, one closer to the center would weaken. This was much more difficult than I had imagined. It quickly became clear that my effort was for naught. My clumsy fingers maneuvered the straw in no apparent order. The farther I progressed with the hat, the more obvious its failure became. As they looked on, three generations of native Panama-hat weavers began laughing, first with their eyes, then out loud. Finally I gave up and joined in. My Panama hat looked more like the Panama Canal.

CHAPTER NINETEEN

ITALIAN SPECIALTY COOKS

"Where's the next bus for Déleg?" An elderly Indian nodded toward an old green and white school bus precariously parked on a steep hill. The bus, marked Trans Panamericano, departed Azogues in forty-five minutes, more than enough time to get to Filanbanco, a major bank, and exchange dollars for *sucres*. Ecuador's currency continued to lose steam, to the detriment of everyone except foreign travelers. The trip cost less than fifty cents, the driver's helper told me as he wiped a quarter inch of grime from the side of his bus. Decals of Mickey Mouse covered the driver's window.

This was a classic third-class South American bus ride, complete with chickens, goats, buckets of slop, burlap bags full of vegetables, sacks of cornmeal and potatoes, tattered suitcases, crying kids, snoring adults, brash fifteen-year-olds ready to take on the world, and drunken twenty-year-olds who had tried. The bus traveled downhill to the hospital, then began a winding ascent that didn't end until we reached Déleg more than an hour later. The only town we passed, Cojitambo, showed little life and lots of poverty. The dirt road we climbed, just wide enough for the bus, cut through soft forests with lush valleys on the other side. Riders hopped off at their homes along the way, and by the time the road leveled off at this pastoral village high in the Andes, only four of us remained.

During the last few miles, the homes, which by all rights should have been miserable see-through hovels, started to show some measure of prosperity. Some were actually made of brick, while wooden homes showed long and skillful labor, ensuring that each board fit snugly against the next. Doors swung on hinges, and opened and shut with the turn of a knob. Real glass filled the window openings. Coats of paint appeared to have been applied within recent memory. Some homes had fences surrounding them, and gates leading to front doors. It wasn't so much that Déleg displayed wealth, for it didn't; it was the absence of poverty that stood out. Hidden away miles from the nearest outpost, Déleg countered all cultural and economic patterns. The bus circled the plaza, passing some old but sturdy two-story houses, and squeaked to a stop in front of a general store. At an isolated South American town twenty-three hundred miles from the United States, an overhanging sign from Filanbanco boasted COMPRAMOS DOLARES. We buy dollars.

A narrower, less traveled dirt road went off the far end of the plaza. Down it, men walked their oxen, women came to market, and children returned from school. Samuel Guzmán stopped to introduce himself.

"You're from the United States? Really?" He spoke in wonder, as if the king of Spain had just dropped in for a beer. "We've never had anyone from the United States visit here. A lot of our people are there. I have a sister who lives in Brooklyn. The other lives in the Bronx. You're the first person from the United States ever to visit us!" He kept rotating his head in a manner I took to mean that this fact was almost too much to absorb. He led me on a walking tour of town, pointing me out, despite my halfhearted protests, to everyone we passed. "Look! From the United States!"

We sat down in the plaza near the waterless fountain. "The first people from this area went to the United States about 1960. We have electricity here because so many of our people went there. Every five years or so they return, sooner if there's an emergency like a death in the family. Our whole town owes its prosperity to the United States. These cement houses were built with money from your country. We go to Cuenca to cash our checks from the United States. We used to get our water from wells and keep it in barrels. Now, thanks to money sent from the States, we have water in pipes."

We returned to Samuel's house, where he maintains a bicycle repair shop. "Right now," he said, motioning to his barren workbench, "there are none to repair." American Airlines posters promoting San Francisco, Los Angeles, and Disneyland hung on a wall. A calendar seven years out of date was tacked up next to them, and beneath it rested a Chevrolet cap alongside a *sombrero de paja toquilla*. His wife sat weaving a Panama hat the whole time. Each time I addressed her, Samuel cut her off and responded in her place.

"To go to the United States we use a system of *falsificando*," of forgery. "There's a travel agency in Cuenca that helps us. It costs three thousand dollars and more. We have to supply photographs and go to Guayaquil. Then we go by plane to Mexico, and cross over from there." He withdrew from the room to get a flier from the travel agency. "Usually after two or three years there a man will send for his wife and the rest of his family."

We began walking again. Another COMPRAMOS DOLARES sign hung above a small store. Everyone seemed to have family in the country one continent away, and rushed to show me the return address on recently received letters. With Samuel heralding my stroll through town, word traveled faster than I did. Soon every mother was waiting in front of her house, ready to stuff an envelope in my hand as if I were collecting entries in the Publishers Clearing House sweepstakes.

Samuel took me to the one place in town to eat. I reached for the doorknob, which turned out not to be a doorknob at all but a cluster of flies so thick they appeared a solid mass. Soup and rice were being prepared. "We don't open for another half hour," the proprietress said. She turned to light a gas burner beneath a pot of brown sludge on which more flies were resting. "What kind of soup will you be serving?" I asked. "Oh, I don't know. Whatever is in that pot."

"I spent some time in the United States," Carlos Vélez Flor, the local political chief, told me. "We all did. All five of my children now live there. Our grandchildren are U.S. citizens! I came back a few years ago because I had arthritis." Samuel interrupted to announce for the tenth time that I was the first *norteamericano* to visit Déleg. "Well," Carlos responded, "once we had a Peace Corps volunteer from Azogues come up to help us build our potable water system."

Dora Vélez, Carlos' wife, is the postmistress. Her domain includes about nine thousand people. Wearing dark eye shadow and black clothes, she looked like a blind woman in mourning. Mail arrives twice weekly in Déleg, she explained, at eight Wednesday mornings and at nine on Sundays. "The post office is very crowded when the mail comes in. We get about three hundred letters from the United States every week. They take about half a month to get here. The majority of them are certified, which means they have money inside them. I've seen checks arrive here for two thousand dollars."

After they get to New York, most of the Déleg men head for an employment agency on West Fourteenth Street between Fifth and Sixth Avenues, where they find work washing dishes or busing tables in Italian restaurants. Weekday mornings, the front room of this agency is filled with Ecuadorans, a handful of whom invariably come from Déleg. Despite their undocumented status, they become certified by the U.S. Department of Labor for jobs that can't be filled through normal means—in their case, "Italian Specialty Cook." In New York, Déleg men live under the rubric of Italian Specialty Cook even if they're only mopping the kitchen floor. Armed with their Labor Department documents they return to Ecuador, where the U.S. Consulate in Guayaquil is obligated to grant them visas to return to the States—this time, legally. It's a tradition.

"We've asked them how they prepare Italian foods like spaghetti or ravioli," a worker in the consulate visa section said, "and they look at us blankly. They have no idea what we're talking about. The damn thing is that with the Labor certification we have to grant them a visa even if we *know* the whole thing's a scam, and then after a while they send for their families. The ones who've never been to the United States before are worse. When we ask where they plan to live, they say, 'Oh, the New York Sheraton.' They've never been outside Déleg in their lives, and all they know is that Sheraton is the name of a hotel. When we ask what they do for a living they say 'businessman.' What kind of business? 'Oh, a merchant.' What kind of merchandise? It turns out they're street vendors or they sell potatoes at the market. A lot of them, when we ask why they want to visit the United States, they say '*Quiero conocer Disney World.*'" I want to know Disney World.

A young man sat behind me on the bus from Déleg back to Azogues. His shirt, recently pressed, was neatly tucked into his polyester slacks. His shoes were shined and his combed hair was still damp from a recent washing. A small and ancient suitcase rested on the floor beside him. "I'm going to Guayaquil," he said, "and then, God willing, to the United States." He spent the whole trip gazing out the back window.

CHAPTER TWENTY

ROMANCING THE HAT

Panama hat sales at Resistol Hats in Texas had not kept pace with the company's growth. With the retirement of Irving Marin, the company's straw-hat expert, there was no one left who had ever been to Ecuador to meet the exporters face-to-face and see the supply line firsthand. Ever since 1952, when Resistol first sold straw hats, it had prided itself on how well received its product had become. Sales were not improving, however, and problems kept recurring with the hats received from South America. Orders came in the wrong style, size, or grade. Hats arrived too late, too early, too many, or too few. On occasion Resistol received hats it had never ordered. Rarely did the right number of requested hats arrive on schedule. The hats that did arrive fluctuated in quality. Often ten percent of a shipment failed to meet in-house standards. They became "throwouts." Paperwork between the two countries sometimes went awry. Orders and confirmations in one country weren't entirely understood in the other. At company headquarters in Garland, Texas, the international letter-of-credit system wasn't entirely clear; the exporters in Cuenca couldn't make themselves understood. Resistol took little consolation that its competitors were likewise suffering.

The entire production system went far smoother with imitation Panamas from the Orient. They looked as good and caused far fewer headaches than the real thing from South America. And they cost substantially less to manufacture—savings that were passed on to customers. Only the discerning shopper could tell the difference between a natural straw Ecuadoran hat and one made from paper product in Taiwan or China. "The paper Panamas have an even weave and a more consistent color," explained Tommy Massie, a wiry Oklahoman who manages Resistol's straw plant. "But they don't breathe, and they wear out after a couple of years." Ecuadorans prided themselves that Panamas were seen around the world on the heads of officials at the 1984 Olympic Games in Los Angeles, unaware that the hats were not made of *paja toquilla* at all but rather were imitations from the Orient. "It's like polyester versus cotton," said Massie, who oversaw the Olympic headgear production. "But not as many people are willing to try the cotton." Impressing the prestige of a genuine Ecuadoran Panama upon the buyers for many retail sales outlets had become more and more difficult for hat companies' sales representatives.

"The hat buyer for most department stores is a twenty-four-year-old girl with no experience who's waiting on a promotion. She thinks she knows hats because her father wore one. But the buyer usually doesn't know the first thing about hats." That's the opinion of Mike Gibbons, Resistol's president until fall 1985, when Levi Strauss sold the company to a Virginia hat-company owner named Irving Joel. "We want to impress our Montecristis upon them," Gibbons said. "The problem is that all of our finest are allocated before the straw-hat season even begins. We can only get so many each year, and while the demand increases, the supply doesn't. There are certain things that will never be assumed by machines. The weaving of a Panama hat is one of them."

Gibbons went to a major New York hatter on Madison Avenue and listened while a sales clerk explained a hat to a customer. "She said it was one hundred percent beaver, and that they only use the finest beaver skins from Europe. Then she said you could tell it's a high-quality beaver hat by the way it snaps back to form if you twist it a little. Finally she told him how good it looked on him.

"Well, she was a hundred percent wrong. First, it wasn't a beaver hat at all. Second, beaver skins don't come from Europe. And third, twisting it a little isn't going to tell you if it's beaver or not. Anyway, the fellow believed everything she said and bought the hat for ninety dollars. We want our sales force in the field to be able to explain the story of the Panama hat to the retail buyers. We want to give it a mystique. Intrigue. That's really what our sales people are doing—romancing the hat."

Gibbons sent Massie from the straw plant and Al Luiz, vice-president in charge of manufacturing, to Ecuador to learn more about the hats and look over the supply line to see if they could resolve some of the problems. "Is their system of pricing different from ours?" Gibbons asked before they left. "How do they block their hats? Are we making unreasonable demands on them? We think that they ship bad hats all the time. They think we bitch all the time. As for quality, when we say we want X, does our X mean the same as their X? Do they want their delivery schedule spaced out? Do they want more lead time or less?"

The two company representatives had their own private thoughts about how Resistol was meeting the Panama hat market. Luiz wore a spiffy Ecuadoran straw hat, shaped safari style. Stetson had beaten them badly with the same style by arranging to call theirs the Indiana Jones model, named after the movie character whose manic devotion to hats became a Hollywood trademark. "When we introduced this style a while back, Mike said the only way this hat is going to die is if we kill it. Well that's exactly what our sales force did, but it was the most popular hat on the market with the competition. It looks good on either sex, at any age, and with any complexion."

"We're killing ourselves by not adapting," Massie added. "Dress and fashion hats are coming back faster than the western ones, and we're turning out the same design year after year. We're not changing a thing. We should."

The two flew to Quito, then on to Cuenca, and sat down with their major supplier, Gerardo Serrano. "We consider you the best company," Serrano said. "When we get hats that we know you want, we hold on to them for you. We don't send them to Stetson or Miller Brothers or any of our other accounts. We save them for you." Silent pride settled over the room before Serrano delivered the punch line: "We only ask that this attitude be reciprocated."

Luiz and Massie shifted in their seats. "Of course," the exporter continued, "you must consider some tolerance in the quantity and quality. We'd prefer it if you didn't order in too large a quantity, and that you require just two grades at a time. The risk you are taking in buying high-quality hats must be taken into consideration. Remember, these are handwoven. For our highest quality hats we have a selected group of weavers to whom we give *toquilla* straw and a block to shape the hat on. To these weavers we advance money for the hats."

The two spent time with their second biggest supplier, Kurt

Dorfzaun, a German-born businessman who has spent most of his life in Ecuador. "Now tell me," Dorfzaun said after the three had talked hats, "what is it with my uncle? Is there a problem?" Karl Dorfzaun, Kurt's elderly uncle, represents his nephew in the United States from his midtown Manhattan office on Broadway. Importers who buy from Kurt in Ecuador must go through Uncle Karl, who relays purchase orders to South America and receives Kurt's shipments from Ecuador to pass on to the buyers. Customers find him a constant source of frustration, a fact Kurt had been only dimly aware of. "Well, yes," Luiz answered diplomatically. "We don't seem to be able to get our orders adequately filled."

One morning they met with Moisés Bernal Bravo, another of the exporters who earlier had explained his operation to me. Next the Resistol representatives went to his archrival and brother Eloy, the *patrón* and major employer in Recaurte. Virtually the entire town turned out to greet the visiting dignitaries from *gringolandia*.

"It means so much for them to see you," the heavyset Eloy told his guests as the welcoming party noisily crowded around to shake hands. "To know someone is there to receive the hats at the other end will help morale tremendously."

"It's quite an education for us to see them all," replied Luiz, startled by the crowd. "We're honored to be here."

CHAPTER TWENTY-ONE

TRAVAILS

The weavers whose hats end up with Serrano, Dorfzaun, or the other exporters are not paid a whole lot more for their work today than they were ten, fifteen, or twenty-five years ago. Despite tentative attempts to form a syndicate of weavers, none has proven successful in the face of the *perros, comisionistas,* and export factories. Government agencies, both provincial and central, have made occasional efforts to help, but like the weavers' stabs at unionizing, little has materially improved their lot. In a cottage industry such as the weaving of Panama hats, the industry regulates the cottage.

Dr. Luis Monsalve Pozo, 1944: "Thousands of hands, white, smooth, fine hands of women, girls' hands weaving *toquilla* fiber, weave the illusion of obtaining their bread and water, when in reality the illusion is converted to mere *centavos* for them, but for others the conversion is to palaces, Cadillacs, villas, tourism, and other things. . . ." The weavers, Monsalve's essay continued, "are scattered in the cities and in the country. They do not have a spirit of a unified class. They do not recognize their problem; they feel it, they live it, but not even from afar do they presume to resolve it. This lack of a bond among the workers, this lack of a class unity, and this original scattering of themselves, lost in the Andean brambles . . . have contributed to the workers not speaking a word, however angry or admonishing."

For more than fifty pages Monsalve followed his own Panama hat trail. He wrote of "the soil which generously produces the fiber, to our cities, mute witnesses of the pain of the people in the painstaking process of their workmanship . . . until arriving in New York to cover millions of human heads." By the end of his Marxist polemic, Monsalve had used charts, statistics, emotion, taxes, and sales figures to expose the system that sends hats to the marketplace.

He analyzed expenses and profits for the weavers, *perros, comisionistas*, and exporters. The year he published, Ecuador sent 4.3 million *sombreros de paja toquilla* abroad, earning 5 million dollars for the exporters.

By 1953, when Monsalve updated and reprinted his tract, fashions had changed, and overseas hat sales had dropped by almost a million annually. This time the exporters responded with a diatribe of their own, denouncing the author for lying with statistics, misrepresenting costs and inventing profits, and spreading "insulting falsehoods." They buttressed their attack with their own statistics negating Monsalve's claims. It was a ringing defense of that particular brand of capitalism which thrives upon the Panama hat industry. More than half of the fifteen exporters who signed the rebuttal to Monsalve's analysis are still in business today.

Monsalve was not the first of his era to inveigh against the hat industry. On the eve of World War II, in 1939, G. H. Mata wrote a poem of epic proportions titled *Juan Cuenca—Biografía del Pueblo Sombrerero* ("Juan Cuenca—biography of the hat-making people"). The protagonist in this remarkable saga is an Everyman of Cuenca, born into a family steeped in the poverty of El Chorro, the Cuenca neighborhood whose women weave hats and spin cloth. Thick with invective against those who gain by the handicraft of the hat makers, Juan Cuenca rails relentlessly against working conditions and profiteering in the industry. The poem abounds with bitter stereotypes of *perros, comisionistas*, factory owners, and gringos—United States and European—who own exporting firms or who import from abroad. First, Juan Cuenca's parents:

> His father was a hat-maker, poorly paid for piece-work,
> In the house of some gringo *toquilla* hat companies.
> At all hours, poorly fed, pounding his worker's mallet,
> As if he were digging his own grave....
>
> ... the moans of his mother, weaving and weaving,
> blurred her vision....

Juan, meanwhile, worked as a hat finisher, tightening and tying the short straw ends that circle the hat's brim when the weaving is complete.

> Many times the straw, strong and slippery,
> Cut his fingers like a twisting knife.
> Always at the meat of his tired finger,
> Leaving the imprint of fiery, yellow canals ...

Mata goes on to portray the abused weaver who spumes spittle and phlegm after years of contorting her torso over her hat board, leading to consumption and lung disease:

> Fiber which the *chola* weaves,
> weaving tuberculosis and hunger,
> Mixing anemia with the ruin of her body,
> shrinking her thorax ...
> Twisting her spine, always leaning toward her work ...

> *Carloduvica palmata*
> Executioner disguised in white clothing ...
> Exalted assassin of the Brown Virgin of the Rosary
> Wearing a lovely sombrero woven by the hands of a *chola*
> Who dies as she lives.

In the end, Juan Cuenca calls for a syndicate of hat workers, closing with a cry on behalf of "the proletariat of the world."

El Chorro, the same community known for its weaving and spinning, is the stage for *Los hijos* ("The children"), a novel by Alfonso Cuesta y Cuesta. In it a little girl is born whose fate at birth is forecast by her nickname: *la tejedorita*—the little weaver. "'Baby girls are born with *paja toquilla* in their hands,'" observes a neighbor.

"'With the hat already begun!'" another notes.

"'Certainly,'" the first neighbor says, "'it would have been better had it been a man. *Más gana el hombre silbando que la mujer hilando*.'" There's more profit in a man whistling than a woman spinning.

Later in *Los hijos*, during a city-wide competition, each weaver enters her best *toquilla* hat, hoping it will be chosen for the Virgin Mary and baby Jesus. The Church keeps all the contestants' hats for itself to export, and the women talk about how much money the hats will bring:

"'In New York, at least a hundred dollars. And the Fathers need more money.'

"On hearing this, another commented: 'Soon we will see the hats in the movies, on celebrities, on the head of a President or an oil baron.'"

The next day I went to the hospital to learn what was behind all this talk about tuberculosis. Was there really a high correlation between tubercular sickness and Panama hat weaving? Are those spritely straw hats found on models in high-fashion spring and summer advertisements causing pain and suffering among their poorly paid weavers? To find out, I visited the Red Cross on the second story of a downtown building whose first floor was under construction. (South of the equator buildings are constructed from the top down.) To reach the steps to the second floor, the determined visitor had to first circumvent wooden barriers, then tiptoe around wet cement and drying plaster, avoid live electrical wires and nails pointed skyward, and, finally, maneuver up a set of narrow, rubble-strewn stairways that lacked railings and, in some cases, steps. Most of the traffic was headed for the blood bank down the hall. The Red Cross directed me to the tuberculosis hospital. My leisurely look at an innocent hat was turning into a detective story.

"We have virtually wiped out tuberculosis here," said the chief doctor, who began working at the clinic in 1957. "It is true that there was a high incidence of tuberculosis in the more rural hat-making communities. So we did a study at Sígsig, where most people at the time had at least one weaver in the family. It turned out that eighty percent of the people who said they had TB had gone to the coast looking for seasonal work between March and October. In another area of high TB occurrence we found no weavers whatsoever. From this we concluded that the somewhat contorted way in which some weavers sit was not responsible for tuberculosis.

"We found a far higher connection between respiratory illness and people who went through a drastic change of climate twice a year than we did with weavers. It goes back to just after World War II, when the international Panama hat market fell. That brought about new behavioral patterns here in Azuay and Cañar provinces—people from the countryside started moving to Cuenca, and many people began to emigrate to the coast looking for work."

The good doctor backed his claim with impressive statistics. I thanked him for his time, and he gave me a ride back to my hotel. It appeared I was out of the detective business.

CHAPTER TWENTY-TWO

CUY FOR TWO

I had again switched lodging—not because of hospitality pompously proffered, but rather because my new hotel didn't live up to its word. When I checked in I asked the afternoon desk clerk if, like the signs on the door said, the hotel took VISA cards.

"*Sí,*" he replied.

"No," the morning desk clerk said as I tried to check out a few days later. "We don't take VISA cards."

"Well, the other fellow said you do," I protested.

"Sorry, I can't take a VISA card." I went through the same conversation with the hastily summoned assistant manager. "*No,*" he said piously. "There must be some mistake. *No aceptamos VISA aquí.* We never have."

"*Mira,*" I said, ushering him by the elbow to the front door. "Look. What does this say?" I pointed to a credit-card-shaped decal that read ACEPTAMOS VISA. "And this? And this? And this?" So many ACEPTAMOS VISA stickers covered the glass door that you could barely see through it. "And you have the temerity to tell me you don't take VISA cards?"

Cuenca's hotels, like one Ludwig Bemelmans stayed at in Riobamba, appeared to have come out of a story conference of the Marx Brothers. In fact, had this been a movie I would have throttled the assistant manager by his puny little throat till his eyes got beady. Instead, I settled for the inner satisfaction at having caught this duplicitous factotum at his own game. Having made my point, I relented, and we retired to his office where we made amicable payment arrangements. When I left, the porter was busy scraping decals from the front door.

I next moved to the Hotel Crespo, whose rooms overlook the Tomebamba River and whose staff tolerates the whims of foreign

130

travelers. I grew rather fond of the Crespo, and it was from there that an Ecuadoran friend and I went down the street for a dinner of *cuy* at Tres Estrellas. An Andean delicacy, *cuy* is a favorite at countryside *fiestas*.

Cuy is guinea pig, precious little furry animals raised on corncobs, alfalfa, grass, and lettuce, then slaughtered between six months and one year after birth. Its name comes from the squeaky noise it makes: *kwee! kwee!* I had to overcome severe cultural bias before finally agreeing to eat one.

Tres Estrellas adjoins the home of its owner, Victor Toral, who served his first guinea pig in 1953. The restaurant takes up ten rooms of a two-story house, with a small bar near the front door. Each room has one wooden table, large enough for a party of eight or more, and is shut off from the other rooms. Large windows look out from the second-floor dining rooms into the hallway below. Bare light bulbs swing from the ceiling. "People come in for a drink and get rowdy," explained Sr. Toral, motioning to the upstairs dining areas. "So it's better to have private rooms." We chose a downstairs room and ordered *cuy* for two.

Sr. Toral allowed me to watch the cook prepare our meal. On the way back to the kitchen I heard an oddly familiar sound followed by a hollow crash of wood. A couple of teenagers were bowling in the back. The alley they bowled on, imported from the United States, diverted diners while they waited the forty-five minutes or so it takes to prepare *cuy*. Except for occasional sweepings and moppings, the two alleys had not been serviced since their installation in 1962, and the wood was severely warped. Small craters pockmarked the alleys from balls tossed by uninitiated bowlers. Each lane resembled the topography of Ecuador itself, with the volcanic Andes down the middle sloping outward to the jungle and the sea.

While one boy bowled, the other acted as his pinspotter, yelling out the number of pins down, clearing the deadwood, and sending the ball back to the front. The lanes were in such pitiful shape, though, that a ball on a perfect toss for a strike might be diverted by a jagged splinter, a sudden bump, or a gradual slope toward the gutter. Likewise, a ball headed for the side could just as easily crash through the strike zone. Bowlers chose from four balls, each so used and abused over the years that they wobbled rather than rolled toward the pins. Coming or going, a ball might lurch onto the adjoining alley or over toward a dozen chickens who watched the games from inside some cages on the sidelines.

Back in the kitchen, the cook, one of Toral's eleven children, had slit a guinea pig along its guts and cut off its feet. A lengthy pole was stuck through the length of the rodent, mouth first, until it came out the other end, then placed over hot coals for a half hour to forty-five minutes. "It's best to use a wooden poker," the Toral lad said as he slowly kept the spit turning three inches above the heat. "Electric rotisseries with their metal spits don't cook the *cuy* as well." A regional cookbook I picked up had these instructions: "The little animal is roasted and skinned one day ahead of time and marinated with garlic, salt, and seasonings. It is later basted with colored hog fat, and slowly roasted over an open fire. Usually accompanied by specially prepared potatoes called '*ají de cuy.*'" This last item was described as "potatoes cooked together with the head of a guinea pig, and browned with colored lard or hog fat. Adorned with slices of hard-boiled egg."

Finally Sr. Toral brought in our roasted guinea pig and placed it on the table. As large as a rat, its cousin, our *cuy* looked like the victim of a forest fire. It had been sliced across the stomach so that each of us could get half. Short, stubby hairs stuck out through its cooked skin. Tiny pointed teeth gave the dead guinea pig's face a sly grin. I took the rear half.

The skin had ducklike crispness, crunchy but tasteless. Inside, there were so many small bones and so much fat and gristle that finding meat to chew proved difficult. Despite its size, *cuy* is definitely a finger food; forks and knives proved irrelevant. The meat, once I found some, tasted spongy, like overcooked rabbit. Juice oozed from all over; guinea pig is a five-napkin food.

Cuy is a traditional meal at funeral services in some parts of Latin America and plays a role at religious feasts as well. Countryside healers rub a live guinea pig on the afflicted part of an ailing patient so that the malady will be transferred to the animal. In sixteenth-century Quito, the still beating heart of a *cuy* was customarily removed and offered to the sun and the moon as part of the last rites. My guinea pig was no good for either ceremonial or medical purposes. It just lay there as I picked at it.

A loud whistle pierced the air, followed by a man clapping noisily. The bartender hurried out to the hallway and craned his head upward. A convivial patron upstairs was leaning precariously out the window of his private dining room, waving an empty bottle of cane liquor. "*Sí, señor*," the bartender said with a nod. He went back to the bar for a full bottle and rushed upstairs to replenish the whistler's stock. Our bill came to $8.40; $7.50 for two plates of roast guinea pig, and $.15 a shot for the booze with which to wash it down.

CHAPTER TWENTY-THREE

THE 10,000 HATS OF ADRIANO GONZÁLEZ

Adriano González appeared particularly tired when he and his wife arrived to unlock the front door at his place in Biblián at six o'clock Sunday morning. They had returned from a wedding *fiesta* just three hours earlier, and now, after the predawn drive from Cuenca, Adriano faced his most arduous day of the week. He quickly set up a chair for his wife, the table across which business would be transacted, and, most important, a small stool on which he put his briefcase filled with 650,000 *sucres*—almost $7,000—in crisp bills fresh from the bank. Within ten minutes the first woman walked in, her arrival announced by the shuffle of her sandals echoing down the hall. The next weaver, less than five feet tall, had her baby strapped to her back in a shawl. She was followed by a woman shorter still. A low hubbub of Spanish and Quechua flowed forth; it was to rise steadily for an hour or so, and then, with occasional lulls, maintain itself until diminishing into the early afternoon. This Sunday, as every Sunday for decades, the economy of Biblián began and ended at the house of Adriano González.

"How much do you think it's worth?" González asked a weaver who handed him a hat to appraise a half hour later. The line had already curved around the corner down the hallway. "Eighty *sucres?*" she replied (about eighty-five cents at the time).

"Seventy-five," he stated with finality. He looked over the second of two hats she handed him. "Ah, here's one worth eighty." Adriano's wife handed the weaver 155 *sucres* as he reached down to take five hats from the next weaver in line.

"What do you want for these?" he asked the lady.

"Sixty *sucres* apiece," she said with a big smile. He laughed at her preposterous request as he looked each one over. "These get fifty-five each," he said, putting four Panamas to the side, "but this one—this

is what I'm looking for. It is free of the inconsistency of the others."
He held it aloft for the other weavers in line to see, then turned to his
wife. "Sixty for one and fifty-five for four." González tossed the newly
purchased 280 *sucres* worth of hats into the back corner.

Another woman, short and bony, reached the front of the line to
sell her handiwork. "I used to make nine hats a week," she said, "but
now I weave only three. My eyes have grown bad. All of ours do after
years of weaving." She thought her hats, made of coarser straw and
with a looser weave, would fetch sixty-five *sucres* each. She accepted
sixty with equanimity. As he did with all the others, González inquired
about her family's health, recalling the names of her husband, sister,
and five children. The lady made a slight curtsy before departing.

For hours it seemed virtually every woman—and some men—
who lived in the Cantón of Biblián approached Sr. González to sell
him their newly woven hats. At his mercy for their weekly pittance,
they stood in small bunches, some silent, others chattering, a few solemn, and a couple drunk.

I walked around front to get a weaver's-eye view. From their side
of the table, González's slender six-foot frame grew another foot. From
this vantage point he clearly had the upper hand—in fact, he had the
only hand. His eyes, his skin tone, his clothes, his home, his gender, his
vocabulary, his height, his wallet—all these gave him every advantage.
Many weavers chewed raw sugarcane while waiting in line; their teeth,
or what was left of them, were as yellow as the hats. I asked a small
cluster of women how long it had taken them to weave their hats—
how many hours. "Who knows? We don't figure time in hours."

Early mass had let out, and now the line stretched almost to the
door. The two dozen weavers closest to the table crowded around, all
waving their hats under González's nose like frantic floor brokers at
the stock exchange. "I can't use these," González told a woman in her
early twenties. He wore the scowl of a stern father.

"But *señor*, you said last week—"

"If you want to try to sell these in Cuenca next week, go ahead.
But to me they're worth only twenty-five *sucres* each."

"*Señor*," she implored, "you said—"

"You heard me wrong. You must have had too much to drink." In
fact, at nine-thirty on a Sunday morning, she did appear somewhat

intoxicated. "Here. Take these back. Don't bother me anymore." He flashed annoyance for the first time, then regained his composure.

"This straw is worthless," he told one forlorn weaver. "Look at this!" He held up the hat for the other weavers to see. The woman giggled nervously with an embarrassed smile. "On this one the brim isn't wide enough." He pulled out his ruler. "Oh, yes—this one is fine."

The exchange began again: "How much do you think it's worth?" Fifty-five, said the weaver; González countered with fifty. His wife had gone off to the second show at church, and Adriano doled out the *sucres*. In the seconds before his fingers touched the stack of bills, each weaver murmured one last desperate plea for a few extra *sucres*. When small children accompanied their mothers, González gave them each a *sucre*. He encouraged young girls just starting out in the hat-weaving trade by paying them a bit more than the same hat would ordinarily fetch.

A succession of ear-splitting fireworks suddenly erupted down the street, to no one's concern. Whenever González criticized a weaver in front of her *compañeras* for shoddy work, she blushed, more so if her children accompanied her. His appraisal of each hat followed a well-defined pattern: He'd grab the hat from a weaver as he finished with the previous one, hold it up to the light, twirl it around once or twice on the index finger of one hand, "bargain" with the weaver, then toss the hat into the corner. One-sided pleasantries were as much a part of the ritual as the final payment. Every five minutes he would stop to neatly stack and restack the growing piles of hats in the corner. Different grades of hats went into different stacks. Two hats here, five over there, another three on the end stack, and six more in the middle. He accomplished this as deftly as a shell game. Sometimes he tossed them into piles from halfway across the room, usually hitting his mark. His cat lurked in the background, hunting for rodents who found the dry, soft *paja toquilla* an ideal playground.

"This is terrible. It's worthless," he told one weaver. "How about ten *sucres*," she replied with a shy grin, acknowledging her sloppy work.

"Ah, now the brims on these are well done!" he told the next woman as he held them up for others in line to admire. Complimented, the woman blushed as a schoolgirl might at gushing praise from her teacher. As the *comisionista* pulled 130 *sucres* from his open briefcase, the weaver counted with him, by color. Each denomination has a different color, so that nonliterates can count their take-home pay.

Dozens more calmly waited to trade in their creations, talking about each other, their weaving, and the price they hoped to get, God willing, but knew they wouldn't. At the table González berated a middle-aged woman for not doing a better job as she had promised. "If your hats improve, you'll get five to ten more *sucres* for each one. But they must look like this." He pulled out a sample hat. Just then a young boy ran in, excited at having just taken his first communion. González tugged playfully at the boy's hair and gave his mother a few extra *sucres* for the occasion.

"Oooh, my aching back." González stretched his muscles after four hours of leaning over to talk with the sellers. "I think I'll take a break." He walked over and sat down next to me, leaving the patient women waiting. "When they hand me a hat, I look at the tightness of the weave, the quality of the straw, the consistency of the color, the size of the brim, and the size of the crown. All of these things have to be good by themselves and consistent with each other. A coarse straw shouldn't be woven too tightly." Engaging and articulate, González seemed careful not to overstep his role as paymaster of Biblián.

"I'm paying slightly more for hats now because this year's corn harvest is so good. These same people can make one hundred fifty *sucres* a day in the field, plus meals and transportation. That's more than they can make weaving hats.

"Tomorrow I make the rounds selling to the hat factories in Cuenca. I have to have all the figures ready for how much I paid out today. On Thursdays I go back to pick up a check from each one. I get the amount I've paid out today, plus six percent. That's my commission. Six percent for each hat. Why, in *sucres* I'm a multimillionaire!"

The *perros* in the field and on the street corners operate similarly, but with more convolutions in the price. These street-corner dandies clad in ties, clean white shirts, and dark suits with rulers in the breast pockets stop practically every woman who is carrying a newly woven hat. In Biblián, Azogues, Cuenca, and throughout the provinces of Cañar and Azuay, the routine follows a ritual established generations ago. First the weaver suggests a price, then the *perro* makes a face and counters with a price half as big while pointing out some imperfections. They haggle back and forth. Others stand nearby, watching, trying to glean what the *perro* is offering that week. The weaver pulls out a second hat, suggesting a compromise price. The *perro* finds more imperfections. She makes her final offer. He says no and starts to hand it back to her. She either accepts the *perro's* price or moves on. On market day, dejected weavers slowly walk corner to corner, hats in hand. One *perro* noticed me watching. "*Son mal pagadas, las tejedoras,*" he said, shaking his head. The weavers are poorly paid. "They can't even eat on what we pay them. The straw costs them twenty *sucres* each, and I buy the hat for fifty. How can they live on that?" The *perros* themselves receive 5 percent profit from the *comisionista* on each hat they buy.

Mariana Arsiaga, the only woman hat buyer I noticed in the streets, looked scornfully at four hats a *chola* handed her on a street corner in Cuenca. The two dickered, the hopeful *campesina* asking forty *sucres* for each hat, the bullying *perra* offering thirty. "OK, all right. Here. I'll take two at thirty-five and two at thirty-two." The weaver nodded and stuffed 134 *sucres* into a side pocket for her week's work. "These are bad ones," Mariana said, not waiting for the *chola* to walk out of earshot. "I shouldn't have bought them."

A few blocks from the Cuenca hat market an independent *perro* wearing a crooked tie and a soiled jacket stood in a corner buying hats that had been rejected by all the regular *perros*. Two city inspectors came by. The *perro's* corner was too far from the *mercado* and he wasn't part of any established network of *perros* and *comisionistas*. They ordered him to pack up and leave. "I'm only trying to make a living," protested the freelancer.

"Well, you can't make it here. Move on."

"But I'm not doing anything wrong." He hastily put his hats in a burlap sack, preparing to go as he argued to stay. "You can't do this."

"You're blocking the sidewalk with your business. Now get going," barked the irritated officials.

"You have no reason to drive me off." His hats were stuffed in the bag now. "I'm here every week." He walked backward, away from the officials, insisting he was doing no wrong. "I can stay if I want to." He made his final getaway, fading into a crowd of pedestrians crossing the street.

At the Ojeda household in Biblián, Isaura was preparing to take her hats over to González's place. On the way home, she planned to shop at the weekly market. "Of course I go to González. If you live here there's no one else to sell to," she said matter-of-factly. "It's been this way for many years."

"He is one of the exploiters of the poor people," Eulalia offered in a low voice.

When Señora Calderón de Ojeda finally inched her way to the front of the line, González spent little time with her. They exchanged gracious niceties, he paid full price for her hats, and she left. She had received sixty-five *sucres* for each of her hats—the going rate for a well-made *brisa*-style *sombrero de paja toquilla*. The straw for each one had cost her twenty-two *sucres*. For weaving a Panama hat, fifty-one-year-old Isaura Calderón Encalada de Ojeda made forty-three *sucres*—approximately forty-five cents.

The untenable situation Panama hat weavers accepted as part of their lives made me think of "Assembly Line," a short story by B. Traven set in Oaxaca, Mexico. An Indian sat day after day weaving beautiful baskets from local straw, dyed with the colors of nearby insects and plants. Each one took twenty to thirty hours to produce. Although he asked fifty *centavos*—four cents at the time—for each basket when he peddled them at market and door-to-door, he almost always relented: "The prospective buyer started bargaining, telling the Indian that he ought to be ashamed to ask such a sinful price. 'Why, the whole dirty thing is nothing but ordinary *petate* straw which you find in heaps wherever you may look for it. . . . If I paid you, you thief, ten *centavitos* for it you should be grateful and kiss my hand. Well, it's your lucky day, I'll be generous this time, I'll pay you twenty. . . . Take it or run along.'"

Traven's Indian artisan sells his basket. "He had little if any knowledge of the outside world or he would have known that what was happening to him was happening every day to every artist all over the world. That knowledge would perhaps have made him very proud, because he would have realized that he belonged to the little army which is the salt of the earth and which keeps culture, urbanity, and beauty for their own sake from passing away."

By midafternoon Adriano González had bought, both over the counter and from his *perros* in the field, ten thousand hats for the week. Their average cost came to just over 60 *sucres* each. In all, González paid out about $6,300. A son arrived to help the *comisionista* load the hats of Biblián into his Travelall for the afternoon drive back to Cuenca.

CHAPTER TWENTY-FOUR

THE LAST JEWS IN CUENCA

Daniel Kuperman, general manager of the Hotel Crespo, sat stirring his coffee in the first-floor dining room as he talked about the memory of his father and the future of his child. Kuperman's family history takes off from turn-of-the-century Russia, where his grandfather served in the czar's army, then winds through World War II with his father's exploits, and ends in the Shuar Indian country of Ecuador's Amazon basin, where Daniel leads expeditions for small tour groups. "When the pogroms came my grandfather fled Russia and ended up selling fruits and vegetables in Paris, where my dad was born. My father had wanderlust, and when he turned twenty-one he came to Colombia, where he made yarmulkas in a hat factory in Baranquilla. He was Jewish.

"When war broke out in Europe he went back to join the French army." When the German occupation came, he joined the Resistance and went underground. He helped to bomb German convoys. He was a very sentimental man, filled with *patriotismo*. He fought with his heart.

"Toward the end of the war he became exhausted, and decided to return to South America. My dad got off in Guayaquil stone broke. The first night he slept on a bench and covered himself with newspapers. The second day he met a rich man in the streets who said, 'Oh! You are a gringo!' My father was a handsome French gentleman, and he told the man he'd just come from the war. The Ecuadoran lent him some start-up money to open a small restaurant and bar next to the U.S. Consulate. He served Chateaubriand and French wine. It was called Henry's Place. He worked like an animal. Once when he visited Salinas he met a woman named Yolanda on the beach. A year later they were married. Her stepfather was a Polish Jew.

"Eventually my father grew tired of the restaurant and bought a *hacienda* near Ambato, where he grew potatoes. He was a romantic. 'The poor Indians have nothing,' he said. He wanted to give them medicine, books, and clothes. So he spent all his money on the Indians and returned to Guayaquil to open another restaurant, and then a nightclub in Quito called Incas. He hired singers and musicians from all over Latin America. With the money from Incas he opened the Hotel Crillon in Guayquil. Papillon was among his guests—father gave him his bed and food. He also put up Legionnaires who escaped France and helped them get work. He led a crazy life.

"He opened up some more hotels around the country, including one on the coast at Salinas. When my little brother was three, the Communists came from town and told my dad to get out because he was taking their natural resources. They dynamited the beach and scared my little brother to death. Literally. With this a little bit of my dad died too."

A Joan Baez tape came through the hotel's speaker system. "He started to dream again, and formed a joint partnership to run a hotel with the government under Velasco Ibarra. But there was a coup a month later, and the new regime said that the friends of Velasco Ibarra were his enemies. So they took my dad's hotel, all his money, and his property. He lost forty-five years of work that day. A few years later, in 1972, he arranged to buy this place. He died in 1979." Kuperman sipped his coffee for the first time.

"Once I saw him crying because the Arabs had attacked Israel on Yom Kippur. He said, 'How could anyone attack Israel on our most sacred day?' That was the first time I knew I was a Jew.

"I studied for three years at the Colegio Hebrew Union in Colombia. I had my bar mitzvah in Cali, Colombia, when I was eighteen. Sarita, my wife, is a Jewish Colombian. I became secretary of the South American Youth Zionist Federation." A waiter interrupted his twenty-six-year-old boss with a telephone call. Daniel took it on a cordless phone.

"Colombia has a large and active Jewish population. They know about Jewish history there, and about the war with the Arabs. In Venezuela, Peru, Argentina, and Brazil they also know. But here—well, there used to be eight Jewish families in town. Now there are only four. In the past, Kurt Dorfzaun had a seder and we used Haggadahs from Argentina. At another seder my sister, her Catholic husband, and my mom came. I think she's a Yiddish mama. The last time we had a *minyan* in Cuenca was at the bar mitzvah of Kurt's youngest son. I have Spanish, Inca, and Jewish-Russian blood flowing through me. I love my blood.

"It would have been simple to assimilate here. Many have. But inside I have to be Jewish, so it's easier to be Jewish on the outside too. Jewish children here have absolutely no reinforcement outside the home. My son is only eighteen months old, but we light the *Shabbas* candles every Friday night so he'll grow up with the traditions."

At a nearby table, waiters served a small group from Europe their *cuy*. Rather than slaughter and roast guinea pigs in the hotel kitchen, Kuperman orders carry-out from Tres Estrellas. "I have a lake near here, and we import trout from Idaho. I also own a small plot of land on the coast. When I want to get away from everything, I go visit the Shuar Indians in the jungle. I've started a little business guiding tours into the Shuar country. It's pretty rugged. When the Shuar come to town they stay here. I'm like their consul.

"I feel a stronger identity with Jews now than I did ten years ago. I love the idea of Zionism. I want to go to Israel and work there and learn Hebrew. I don't know if I'll stay, but I want to try it. Here, everyone is into drugs, cars, liquor, motorcycles, and so on. If you know anyone in the States who'd like to buy the Crespo, let me know."

The next morning a couple in their fifties sat talking with Kurt Dorfzaun in his office as his staff sorted through the hats left by Adriano González and other middlemen. The couple, a sculptor and his wife, had come to Ecuador two years earlier because of a particular type of rock that lent itself especially well to chiseling. That type of rock was impossible to find in their native Israel. But an Ecuadoran diplomat there had led them to believe that they could set up shop in Ecuador and export works to the United States. Confused, the couple traveled from their rural home near Loja to petition Dorfzaun for aid as if he were the Israeli consul. This was their third visit to his office. The three chatted awhile; had Mr. Dorfzaun found them a studio or a place to live near Cuenca?

He had not, the tall businessman regretted. He had asked around the Rotary Club and among his other friends; no luck. None of the local Jews could help either. The conversation lost its momentum as the Israelis realized that the one man in town they felt comfortable asking for help had run out of possibilities. "Hey," Dorfzaun exclaimed, looking over at me with a smile. "We almost have a *minyan* here!" The mood lightened up somewhat. I admitted I hadn't been inside a synagogue since my bar mitzvah twenty-five years earlier. "He's a *goy*!" Dorfzaun said with obvious glee. "He's a *goy*!" The couple forced a smile, and Dorfzaun ushered them out.

"What can I do in a situation like that?" he asked when he returned. "I tried. But no one had space available. This happens every once in a while—some Jews new to the country will come to me for help. Some I can, others I can't."

Late in 1938, thirteen-year-old Kurt Dorfzaun traveled with his family from Munich to New York and then to Cali, Colombia. "My father had a wholesale drugstore and cosmetics-supply business. He sold it to a man in 1938 who had helped Hitler fifteen years earlier when he tried to overthrow the government. It was this man who arranged for my family's passage out of the country. Most of my cousins, my grandparents, uncles, and aunts were sent to concentration camps. In Colombia my father had a cutlery factory. An uncle of mine had escaped to Ecuador and went into the hat trade. I later joined him and I've been in the hat business ever since." Although many of the European Jewish newcomers were shocked at barefoot soldiers and people picking lice out of each other's hair, an immigrant doctor forged their collective attitude toward their new homeland: "*Ich lebe lieber unter verlausten Menschen, als unter vertierten Menschen.*" I prefer to live among vermin-infested people than among beastly people.

The father of Kurt's wife, Ilse, had been the *shamus* of a synagogue in Essen. In November 1938, all the synagogues in Germany were burned to the ground and Jewish men were taken to concentration camps, their homes burned and the windows smashed in. "They took my father to the synagogue with machine guns. They made him turn on the lights and pour gasoline all over. He was forced to burn everything there." The temple's thirty-six Torahs were burned in the park next door. The family moved from house to house, each time more fearful. Ilse and her parents escaped, joining thousands of others who took refuge from Hitler in Latin America. She met Kurt during Hanukkah in 1952 in Colombia, where he traveled often on business. They were married the following year.

In the mid-1950s Dorfzaun met a German businessman who passed some time in Cuenca visiting a stepson. On a few occasions the businessman joined some of the refugees from his homeland for chitchat at the Cafetería Toledo. "He was looking for Jewish companionship," said Dorfzaun, who sipped coffee with the stranger a few times. Soon the German moved to Chile, but in 1984 his death made international news. He had been Walter Rauff, the Nazi SS colonel who developed the particularly insidious technique of killing victims by stuffing them into trucks disguised as Red Cross vans and asphyxiating them with exhaust fumes. "He used to have many Jews among his friends. In Ecuador, nobody knew about him."

Public-service awards hung on Dorfzaun's office wall, along with a picture of Moshe Dayan and a letter from Princess Diana's Lady-in-Waiting: "Dear Sir: The Princess of Wales has asked me to write and thank you for the handsome Panama hat. Her Royal Highness was grateful for your thought in sending this present and asks me to send her sincere thanks." Dorfzaun chuckles each time he tells about sending the wedding gift to Prince Charles's wife, and how, thinking it was junk mail, he almost tossed out the reply.

The Dorfzaun house sits in a fashionable neighborhood where decades earlier cattle grazed and townspeople collected firewood. Dorfzaun's office, his car, and his home are filled with telephones and other communications gear. From the house he talks with his children in the United States by ham radio. Months earlier he had received Resistol's purchase order on his office Telex, relayed through his uncle Karl in New York. As we drove up to the house for lunch he honked the horn, and the servant came out to open the driveway gate before returning to the stove.

"Can you buy matzo in Cuenca?" I was curious because the first course from the kitchen was matzo-ball soup.

"The law says that you have to pay an import duty to bring bread into the country because we make our own. But we can import matzo duty free." This dispensation raised another possibility: Perhaps I could stay in the Andes and open up—yes! La Matzoría—The Matzo Hut.

Kurt interrupted the fantasy. "Did you see the story about you in this morning's newspaper?" A reporter for *El Mercurio*, Cuenca's main daily, had interviewed me a couple of days earlier. WRITER FROM THE UNITED STATES COLLECTS FACTS ABOUT TOURIST ASPECTS read the headline. The article said that I was writing a firsthand report about human conditions in Ecuador, and in Cuenca I was particularly interested in "all the necessary information about this important region of the country." Dorfzaun invited me to speak to the local Rotary Club, which he helped found. "We meet next Tuesday evening; can you make it?"

Dorfzaun is a *macher con mucha palanca*, a well-connected big shot: "I'm on the local utilities board, which oversees the telephone, electricity, and water works. I came to Ecuador as a foreigner, but now I feel at home. For many years I've been part of the Chamber of Industries. I even served on the Fé Alegría—a Catholic organization. I was its president! They established a school for the poor and hold an annual raffle. After three years as president of a Catholic group, for a Jew—that's enough.

"A while back we built a synagogue on property owned by the Catholic Church. Two days before Rosh Hashanah the Church said we couldn't use it because people would say they rented it for the money. During the Vietnam War we had about ten Jewish boys here in the Peace Corps and five Jewish girls. We held services here at the house every week. We even used prayer books in English."

With a *minyan* no longer likely in Cuenca, the Dorfzauns now fly to Colombia for the High Holy Days, or to Miami. Cuenca's two Torahs, however, still live with the family. "I wanted to send them to the Jewish community in Quito, but the other Jew here said no. So now I keep them here"—he led me to a hiding place elsewhere in the house—"so no Gentiles will handle them." He has also held on to one of the few mementos he carried with him from Germany to the New World: a prayer book given to him for his bar mitzvah inscribed by a family friend, F. Kissinger, uncle of Henry.

The city gave a small part of its cemetery to the local Jewish community in the late 1950s. "Of the thirty or so Jews who came here, most have moved to Guayaquil, Quito, or to another country, or they have died. Many couldn't adapt; they had the Holocaust behind them and an uncertain future in front of them. Jews who fled to New York had community, but in Cuenca they had almost nothing. Some committed suicide. In another generation I'm afraid the cemetery will be all that remains of the Jewish community in Cuenca." Kurt handed me the key to the gate.

The Jews in Cuenca have buried twenty-five of their own within the small cemetery's stone-and-brick walls. Epitaphs were inscribed in Hebrew, Spanish, and German. Recently placed flowers rested against a few tombstones. A family visiting the adjoining municipal graveyard looked over the fence.

CHAPTER TWENTY-FIVE

ASSEMBLY LINE

Cuenca's profoundly religious society began to shift out of low gear in the mid-1960s. Roads to Guayaquil and Quito—unpaved, but roads nonetheless—were not completed until about 1950. A tire factory opened in 1963, followed by ones making ceramics, kitchen equipment, and household furnishings. Suburbs developed, and the city began a transition from a market center for goods from the countryside to one that could support some industry. Cuenca's population tripled during that time. The city is still immersed in that change, but vestiges of a far slower, feudal Cuenca are everywhere. It can be seen at the Tomebamba River, in whose waters mothers still gather every day to wash the family laundry and on whose banks the clothes are spread out to dry. An old riverside mill lies almost directly below the Hotel Crespo. Just down the street, *sombreros de paja toquilla* hang on the walls of a little hole-in-the-wall shop. Similar shops dot Cuenca and smaller towns; I thought that they sold new Panamas.

They don't. They are hat restoration shops for *cholos* and Indians. "People usually own two or three hats," explained Luis Figueroa, a grizzled seventy-four-year-old hat renovator. "They start wearing them when they're very, very young, every day, from the moment they get up in the morning until they go to sleep at night, for the rest of their lives. One of the hats is always in the shop being cleaned and, if necessary, reblocked. Usually they bring one in for a cleaning every few weeks." As he spoke, Figueroa wiped a sticky, glue-like gum over a hat to stiffen the brim. Sunlight sliced through the doorway onto the back wall. A charcoal-heated iron, a wire brush, wooden hat blocks, sulfur, and other tools of the trade lay on his ancient workbench. His customers paid between thirty-five and fifty-five cents for hat restoration, depending on the work required.

Some two thousand hats lay about the little shop his father had started decades earlier.

Across town Adriano González was delivering newly woven hat bodies to the factories of several exporters, who treat the hats before shipping them abroad. By day's end he had unloaded all 10,000 hats with Ortega, Serrano, and the others, including "*el gringo* Dorfzaun," as Kurt Dorfzaun is often called. At each plant, workers started counting the hats right away. The *sombrero* woven by Sra. Calderón de Ojeda in Biblián from *paja toquilla* harvested by Domingo on the coast was one of the 2,068 hats Adriano González brought into the assembly line at Kurt Dorfzaun's factory.

One of Dorfzaun's workers took dozens of hats home with him, Isaura's included, to tighten the straw and trim the edge. When the hats came back the next day, they were put in large vats filled with a bleaching solution. For two or three days the hats soaked in the troughlike vats, after which they were transferred to another vat for further bleaching. When they came out of the second vat, their color was more uniform and they were sundried on the patio in the middle of the plant. Once dry, the hats spent the night in a closet fumigated with sulfur fumes for further bleaching and disinfecting. After that the final half inch of straw was cut from their perimeter.

The Panamas have taken a beating by this time—stretched, soaked, sunned, and snipped. To make the weave more even and the straw more pliable, they were placed on blocks, where the crowns were pounded with mallets and the brims were hand-ironed to ensure a uniform smoothness. After another steaming, each hat got a MADE IN ECUADOR sticker, required by law for exports, attached to the inside crown.

A hundred workers are involved in this continuous flow of hats through Dorfzaun's plant, including those who take the hats home to cut off and tighten the straw. Each worker gets seventeen months' worth of wages yearly; the extra five months include Social Security payments, a bonus month in March, September, and December, and another month spread out over ten payments throughout the year. Additionally, 15 percent of the company's profits must be divided up among the workers. "The national laws say you can't fire a worker after three months," Dorfzaun complained. "If you do you must pay two years' salary." A plant the size of Dorfzaun's must also maintain a small *víveres* outlet of its own. Ecuador's minimum wage, adjusted annually, was set in mid-1985 at eighty-five hundred *sucres* monthly, between eighty and eighty-five dollars. Most of Dorfzaun's workers earn more.

An incentive program at Dorfzaun's plant rewards employees for punctuality. His workers—and Dorfzaun himself—punch in and out on a time clock, an almost unheard-of practice in Cuenca, where work usually gets done *mañana*, tomorrow. "*Mañana* means so much here," Dorfzaun said with a sigh. "It can mean I don't want to do it, I'll do it later, I'll get around to it eventually, or I'll never do it. Only seldom does it mean tomorrow. When I ask somebody to do something and they say, of course, *mañana*, I say, look: Am I paying you today for tomorrow? I told them I don't want to hear that word around here anymore."

Adriano González stopped by that Thursday to pick up his check for the 2,068 hats he had brought by at the beginning of the week. The hats had cost him 124,290 *sucres*, to which Dorfzaun added in a 6 percent commission of just under 7,500 *sucres*. Adriano González made slightly less than $80 for buying hats in Biblián and delivering them to Kurt Dorfzaun. Altogether, he made about $400 that week from all the Cuenca export factories.

Once the hats had been grouped by size, style, color, and destination, they were tightly packed twenty dozen to a sack. Although some stayed in the country for sale at boutiques and gift shops, most were to be shipped elsewhere in Latin America, and to North America, Europe, and Japan. The six thousand hats destined for the Resistol Hat company in Texas were to go first to Uncle Karl in New York. Kurt charges thirty-six dollars a dozen for *brisa*-style hats. After having gone through the rigors of a hat factory, Isaura's hat now costs three dollars.

Money from Uncle Karl in New York does not go directly to his nephew's bank account. Instead, it has to go first to the government's Banco Central, which must collect from the foreign bank against which the check is written before the exporter gets his money. No interest accumulates during the six weeks and more that it takes for the foreign checks to clear. When Dorfzaun finally collects, he receives payment in *sucres* at the Banco Central rate, which lags about 20 percent behind the floating rate used in most domestic transactions. If, for example, Dorfzaun's check from New York came to five thousand dollars, he would instead receive the *sucre* equivalent of slightly more than four thousand dollars. The hats González brought in from Biblián that week were among the 384,000 Panama hats Kurt Dorfzaun exported that year.

Before leaving Cuenca I went to see the Ojeda family in Biblián one last time. Surprised at my visit, Isaura offered the ultimate compliment: "If I'd known you were coming, I'd have baked you a *cuy!*" Talk at the Ojeda house centered around Isaura's son-in-law, an agronomist who had gone to the United States. He had written from Brooklyn that he had found work in a supermarket. His wife and son hoped to join him within a year. "But we'll go with visas," María Elena said. "I understand for a woman and a child it can be dangerous to go the other way."

When hats from Biblián were first exported in the nineteenth century, Manuel Alfaro, father of the Liberal revolutionary, took them by ship to Panama. Until air service from Ecuador became reliable in the late 1950s, Dorfzaun's hats were always sent by mail from the Cuenca post office and put on a freighter in Guayaquil. A few months later they'd arrive in New York. Now hats going to the States are brought across the street to the bus terminal for shipment to Guayaquil, where they're put aboard an Ecuatoriana Airlines flight to New York.

PART THREE

CHAPTER TWENTY-SIX

DEAD DRUNK

The hats weren't quite ready to take off for the United States and I wasn't either. I suppose I could have waited around Cuenca, then joined them for the ride to Guayaquil and booked a seat on the same flight north—but the truth is I couldn't bear to leave South America right away. I might never again get this close to the Incas, the Andes, the Amazon, and the equator. For all its frustrations and exasperating customs, Ecuador had its hold on me. I had time for one final sweep through the country, visiting places I'd missed so far.

My last swing began at Pujilí (poo-hee-LEE), a town in the central highlands at the base of Cotopaxi, the volcano south of Quito. A few weeks earlier I had met a ceramist from there named José A. Olmos and ordered some custom-made figurines from him. He suggested I pick them up on the day of the Corpus Christi *fiesta*, a traditional festival born of that curious amalgam of pre-Columbian ritual and post-Columbian colonialism, with a wafer-thin layer of Catholicism on top. It started as the most bizarre celebration I'd ever witnessed and ended as the most tragic.

A mile-long parade dominated the day, beginning after church services and winding through Pujilí for an hour until it passed the reviewing stands at the main plaza, where dignitaries watched the gala procession. What was once a special day for Indians from the surrounding countryside to move at will through the town had become an established civic event borrowing heavily from Indian customs and symbols. Everyone looked forward to the festivities, including the traffic cop five miles east of town who stopped the bus I rode and demanded twenty *sucres* from the driver before we could push on.

Danzantes, dancers, play the most prestigious role in the celebration after the *prioste*, the organizer who leads the hundred or so entries in the parade. Rare and colorful, brazen and gaudy, *danzante* costumes are painstakingly pieced together for months before the *fiesta*. A hodgepodge of trinkets—beer cans and mirrors, ribbons, cigarette packs, and other baubles—are fastened to a rectangular cloth lined with aluminum foil. The cloth, or *cola*, hangs from the back of an elaborate headdress jingling with coins, cheap jewelry, and beads. As part of his tinseled regalia, one *danzante* displayed pheasant feathers and a framed picture of a dog clipped from a magazine. Across the back of another lay a rabbit skin with tiny battery-operated light bulbs flashing in its eyes. A third *cola* sported a noisy wind-up alarm clock and dolls—blond, blue-eyed, and naked. Boys aged eight and up danced in white costumes with pillowcase hoods. These *diablillos*, little devils, pranced about, set off fireworks, and good-naturedly harassed onlookers. One ran up to a man about to take his picture, covered the camera lens with his hand, and demanded money. The photographer laughed, handed the kid some *sucres*, and snapped away. An alpaca clad in silk carried a wreath on its head, and on its back, a blond-haired plastic baby Jesus. A military band with indigenous flutes and pipes entertained; their music sounded as if John Philip Sousa had visited the Andes.

Each entry in the parade represented a school or a club, a neighborhood or a town; participants came from villages throughout the highlands. Sometimes a family or simply an individual would join the procession. The *diablillos*, some of whom carried whips and used stockings to obscure their features, mimicked onlookers, ordering people around in falsetto. These mischievous devil-spirits zigzagged through and around the parade mocking Spaniards and the white elite. One group staged a play lampooning authority as it marched through the streets shoving *campesinos* around. A visiting lad wore a gorilla mask and full military uniform; another romped in a Bozo the Clown outfit. Yet another made fun of *costeños* by carrying big bunches of bananas. He was followed by a man in a Chaplinesque Hitler-face who led some teenagers prowling about in drag, hairy legs protruding from beneath their dresses. One boy in sunglasses played with his falsies, much to the crowd's delight, then hiked his silk skirt thigh-high. The next group acted out *Little Red Riding Hood*, accompanied by a man hoisting a painting of the Big Bad Wolf in Grandma's bed.

Civic bands, their musical selections often at odds, raced through their repertoires. The national police from Riobamba sent a thirty-five-piece ensemble. Speakers on cars sandwiched between the bands blared Latin pop from cassette players and radios. Shimi-Aya, folkloric musicians from Ambato, had started drinking early and kept bumping into one another as they walked down the street playing highland instruments and pounding hairy drumskins. What sounds these drunkards coaxed from their wooden flutes! One musician rattled a curious instrument assembled from tin, wires, and springs. It sounded like crickets at dusk. All up and down the route, strangers shared glasses of *aguardiente* and bowls of chicha, a drink made from masticated and fermented corn.

A master of ceremonies excitedly welcomed each group as it passed the reviewing stand. A few men paraded by in white pants and shirts, lifting mannequins of saints whose faces were covered with gauze. Giant Indian scarecrows propped up on poles were carried throughout the parade. The marchers passed faded posters from defeated political campaigns peeling from the buildings. One called for UNITY OF ALL THE PEOPLE; another, with a sketch of Che Guevara, urged NATIONAL LIBERATION AND SOCIALISM. The parade offered an opportunity to petition the authorities for improved living conditions. One man solemnly walked alone, carrying a sign asking for water and electricity. He kept his eyes straight ahead through the entire route, not even acknowledging periodic cheers from the crowd. Just before he reached the reviewing stand, the cellophane tape on his placard weakened and his sign hung askew. When he passed the finish line, the announcer enthusiastically read his plea over the public-address system; whistles and applause filled the plaza. "And *señor*," the breathless announcer proclaimed, "You shall get these things!" A thousand people cheered his false promise. The man walked on.

A four-foot-tall woman wearing two shabby fedoras insisted I drink from her cup of *chicha*. Her bare feet were grossly enlarged from a lifetime of nothing between them and the ground. A sip of *chicha* convinced me that it was superior to *pulque*, the phlegmlike Mexican drink made from the maguey cactus. I broke away before she could offer me more and found a group from Cañar, the province that includes Biblián. Broad white felt hats covered their heads, blood-red ponchos covered their white shirts and pants. Playful Indians with painted-on mustaches and beards followed, and after them a group holding aloft a wooden platform on which rested a bottle of whiskey and a lemon. Their leader, in a clown outfit and dunce cap, walked over to offer spectators some *aguardiente* from a wooden cup that had just made the rounds of his group. I politely declined. "But sir," he said, "won't you have a *copa de ruina?*" A cup of ruin. Two men playing metallic flutes decorated with cigarette packs came next.

"*Pssst, señor—un tango?*" A sip. "*Una copita?*" All day long friendly people offered me drinks from their home brew. "Shall I dip my cup for you?" This particular man carried a pail of *chicha*. After each stranger swallowed a *trago*, the man returned to his spot on the curb and cleaned the cup by dipping it in a vat of rinse water and drying it with his sleeve. Then he offered more *chicha* to the next fellow.

Two men rode side by side on horseback holding a long pole between them. Live roosters hung from the pole, tied by their feet. An itinerant photographer set up his camera in the plaza displaying dozens of pictures in which no one smiles. Next to the photographer sat a mother nursing her baby boy. Her two daughters busied themselves delousing each other's hair. One woman set up a stand to sell grapes and strawberries; another served Ecuador's national dish, *papas con papas*—potatoes with potatoes. Boys wearing chaps rode ponies, somber men in gray suits walked in formation, girls in stylish waist-length ponchos giggled by, and a boy clutching a bottle of *aguardiente* shouldered some fruit that had empty Jell-O boxes tied to it. The parade was full of oblique symbols and derision, joyful sacrilege and desecration.

I ran into Sr. Olmos, the ceramist, on his way home from the parade, and we went to his studio a few blocks from the plaza. I had requested that he sculpt a few writers and photographers, some male, some female. I left to him what they were to be doing and what they should look like.

All figures were European-looking with styled blond hair. They stood four inches tall, colored with enamel paint. The women wore full-length dresses, and the men, checked shirts and Edwardian jackets. The writers held pens, actually tiny tacks, and wrote on copies of newspapers that Olmos had dated Corpus Chirsti Day. The photographers—how did he know?—were obnoxiously thrusting their cameras forward, as if into some unwilling subject's face.

The crowd drifted from the plaza to a dirt field a few blocks away, where cooperatives and neighborhood groups had erected poles about thirty feet high, topped with wooden frames from which hung prizes for the masses. Each pole was supposed to be rooted at least three feet into the ground. To get at prizes, all the young boys had to do was shinny up the poles. The catch was that the poles were thoroughly greased. Those who reached the top were rewarded with toys, pots and pans and other kitchen utensils, clothing, fruit, beer and liquor, and items useful around the house. Suspended from a few of the *castillos*—castles—as they are called, were live sheep, rabbits, and guinea pigs. The animals had been tied by their feet and hung upside down, swaying in midair.

By late afternoon the happily sotted crowd engulfed each pole while determined kids, intoxicated with booze and bravado, climbed closer and closer to the tops before sliding back down. Eventually enough boys had tried the dozen poles that most of the grease had begun to wear off; one by one each castle was scaled, and its prizes tossed down to dozens of arms straining upward to snare a gift. Two, sometimes three, boys at a time tried each pole.

One particularly challenging pole induced about ten boys on it, each resolved to reach the top. With so many bodies shinnying up it, the pole quivered, then began a barely perceptible wobble, and slowly circled wider and wider. Dozens of people below, hungry for free knickknacks, ignored the impending disaster and kept yelling encouragement to their favorite sons. Finally the pole swayed so widely that it passed the point of no return. The crowd shrieked in horror. Terror covered the boys' faces. Some leaped desperately into the panicky mob. Others stayed put, wrapping their arms and legs around the failing pole. The pole seemed to descend in slow motion, as if to give everyone time to prepare for his fate. For one brief moment after it hit the ground, the world was silent. Then pandemonium reigned.

"*¡Dios mío!*" wailed a woman. My God! "What has happened?"

"My son!" sobbed another. "Where is he?"

"Everyone's dead!"

Small children cried. Ice cream vendors renewed their chant:

"*¡Helados! ¡Helados!*" Prayers in Quechua and Spanish floated up.

"They're supposed to limit these poles to three boys and no more," said an angry man. "Why did they let so many get on?"

"Quick! Get them to the clinic!"

"Four of them died," claimed a man who knew nothing more than the rest of us. "Of that I am certain."

Lifeless bodies were crammed inside a makeshift ambulance. Musicians continued playing songs where they had left off.

A crowd formed around the fallen pole, inspecting its jagged end. The part that remained rooted appeared no more than a foot in the ground.

Friends and next of kin traded nervous words outside the Pujilí clinic, where some fifty people crowded around the door. "The two most seriously injured youths were taken to the hospital at Latacunga," said a nun wearing a beatific smile. "At Latacunga," twenty minutes away, "they may get better treatment."

Then again, they may not. Either way, as I recounted the tragedy in the days that followed, I was assured that if any of the boys had indeed hemorrhaged to death, which seemed very probable, they were the lucky ones, because now they didn't have to grovel and suffer for the rest of their lives, and they probably went straight to heaven because they died during the Fiesta de Corpus Christi. Their families now had one less mouth to worry about feeding, and only one more tombstone to lay flowers upon—in all, a considerable savings.

Dios mío.

CHAPTER TWENTY-SEVEN

CRUISING WITH OLGA

After the tragedy at Pujilí, I returned to Quito where I visited with Olga Fisch, at whose *artesanía* shop some of Kurt Dorfzaun's finest Panama hats were sold. One of the unacknowledged facts in the *artesanía* trade in much of Latin America is that without the admiration and marketing skills of North Americans and Europeans, many handicraft skills would be virtually lost to us now. Indigenous products in Ecuador, like the people who make them, have generally been of little interest to the rest of the country. Most of the shops and galleries—in the folklore trade the two are often the same—are run by or cater to people from other continents. Hungarian-born Olga Fisch, one year younger than the twentieth century, pioneered this phenomenon. Since 1943, four years after she took refuge in Ecuador from the war in Europe, her shop, Folklore, has developed an international reputation for its wide assortment of indigenous arts and crafts. Collectors and researchers from abroad visit frequently to pay homage. The Smithsonian Institution regularly seeks her advice and exhibits her collections, including her priceless Corpus Christi dance costumes. Through her knowledge of Indian customs and her close association with their practitioners, she has become the grande dame of Ecuadoran folk art. Still spry and alert, Olga Fisch received me at her home behind the shop.

She is a pack rat of the highest order. Works from four centuries line the walls of her house, from imitation Spanish religious art dating back to the late 1500s in Quito to hand-carved musical instruments made recently in the highlands. Woolen rugs, for which she is especially known, employ her original patterns based upon subtle and handsome elaborations of native designs in painting, pottery, and textiles. They are made exclusively for her, and can be identified by o. FISCH woven into a corner.

We sat on a patio lined with exotic flowers and vines, facing a tidy garden where a barefoot Indian shoveled dirt. Her silver hair had been treated to a permanent, and her right hand sported a turquoise ring from New Mexico. She lighted a Marlboro and poured some Kirsch of Eger, a liqueur from Budapest.

"Where shall I begin? My first trip to South America was aboard the Graf Zeppelin in 1935. I was the first woman to ever ride it across the Atlantic. They made a big fuss about me when we landed in Rio. I had been an artist in Hungary, Austria, and Germany, then Morocco and Italy. When my husband and I were forced to leave Europe for good because of the Nazis, we went to the United States, where the immigration officials told us the quota for Hungarians was filled for the next eighty-six years. They had forgotten the words to their national anthem, 'sweet land of liberty.'

"We spent a year in limbo in New York. While I was there I was offered a job at *Vogue* magazine paying four hundred dollars a week. In 1938! I couldn't take it because we had to leave the country. We decided on Ecuador after hearing about it from friends and seeing pictures of it in a book at the library. We took a ship, then came overland to Quito.

"Pardon me. I have to give something to my *viejo*." She called over to the gardener. "Manuel? Would you like your drink now?" He smiled and bowed slightly.

"Ah, sometimes it is so difficult to find the right employees," she said after pouring a noonday shot of vermouth for her gardener. "There are three ways of doing things: the right way, the wrong way, and the South American way. I suppose I have been lucky. I've had five cooks in forty years. Each has raised a child with my support. I've had to teach each one how to cook Hungarian dishes, and I am such a bad cook myself." A long-distance call came for Olga. Erlinda, the current cook and house servant, walked over to hand her *patrona* the cordless telephone.

"Anyway, a little while after we arrived here I got a job teaching art. I was paid eighteen dollars a month. The people here didn't know what a Jew was. One of my students asked, 'Are you a Protestant Jew or a Catholic Jew?' I started going out to the countryside to see the folk art and meet the Indians, and I gave in to my impulse of collecting everything that appealed to me. And that's what I've been doing ever since."

Erlinda called us to lunch: brisket of beef, spinach, yucca root, and bean salad. "Here, try some *maracuya*. It's a passion fruit, almost like marijuana."

Her mention of marijuana allowed me to ask about a psychedelic from the Amazon: "Have you ever tried *ayahuasca?*"

"Once, yes. I had the feeling that one leg was way up here, and the other was *way* down here." She waved her hands slowly up and down. "I only had a little, but I couldn't walk from here to there," she said, indicating a distance of ten feet. We concluded the meal with a sweet Hungarian wine, Tokaji Szamorodni. "I get it from someone at the Hungarian Embassy," she said impishly. "Now, please. It is time for my nap. Can you come tomorrow for breakfast?"

The next morning the watchman let me in the back door and I was taken upstairs to Olga's bedroom, where Erlinda brings breakfast and *El Comercio* while *la señora* barks out orders for the day to her staff. Morris, a middle-aged Swedish expatriate, joined us. Guerrilla activity in the Peruvian Andes dominated the newspaper's front page.

"Ecuador is like an island in South America." Olga boasted of her adopted country. "It is very peaceful."

"Yes," Morris added, "but sometimes there is trouble even on islands." When I related my impressions of Cuenca's rigid class structure and its "nobles," he nodded. "They fancy themselves as *puro castellano*," purebred Spanish, "but everybody has a little tarbrush on them. They all have some Indian blood but they refuse to acknowledge it."

"There is a legend about how the 'Cuencano type' evolved," said Olga, warming to the subject. "Many years ago a governor of Azuay Province had a Czechoslovakian wife. She slept with their Indian servant, and the result was the Cuencano type. I love Cuenca and its people, but the upper class is rather inflated, isn't it?"

Just then Erlinda entered with our breakfast. Olga erupted. "Why are you a half hour late?" she yelled. "You know I eat at seven-thirty sharp. I have guests! Now put the tray here on my bed." Accustomed to such tirades, Erlinda bowed her head slightly and murmured apologies before quickly retreating. The outburst was as surprising for its trilingualism as for its abruptness, because it came in Spanish, Hungarian, and English. A twinkle crept into Olga's eyes as Erlinda descended the stairs. "I do have these explosions," she admitted quietly, "but I will never get an ulcer. I always let out my anger."

"Then she returns to her sweet self," Morris added benignly.

"For my worst words I use Hungarian. No one can understand me then."

A problem had developed over a carpenter's work on a downstairs door. "It has taken him so long. On the salary I pay my workers they all go to the university, and then I have to adjust their work assignments to fit their class schedules. It's crazy, ¿no?"

One reason Olga's shop has maintained it reputation over the years is her periodic trips to indigenous villages. Her contacts among the Indians in small towns were so legendary that I suspected it was more myth than fact. El Día de San Juan, Saint John's Day, was upon us, and Olga offered me the opportunity to test the legend. "I'm getting too old to drive. Would you like to come with me this Sunday to look for *fiestas* in Imbabura Province? There are supposed to be some near Otavalo."

The Volkswagen bug proved easy to maneuver around church traffic, and soon we were motoring through the Andes along the two-lane Pana, as the Pan American Highway is called, nearing the town of Cayambe. Whenever we asked about *fiestas* that day, however, people would reply that there was certainly one a few towns away, but never in their own village. When we arrived "a few towns away," we'd get the same response. We felt as Alice must have in *Through the Looking Glass* when her repeated attempts to climb a hill always brought her back to the beginning.

"Pull over there," Olga instructed as we skirted Cayambe. "Over to that lady." She rolled down her window to speak to a woman who wore a dark blue shawl around her head. "Excuse me, *señora*. Your blouse— it is from Zuleta, ¿no?" Zuleta is a town on the *hacienda* of Galo Plaza, Ecuador's president between 1948 and 1952, who remains the country's bona fide international statesman.

"Why, yes it is," replied the woman, surprised and flattered that this elderly European lady could pinpoint the origin of her clothing. "I am from there. Yes."

"I thought so. I could tell by the embroidery."

By noon we had struck out, and we stopped for a bite in a restaurant at Lake San Pablo. In the distance a family fished for its dinner from a canoe. "You see that mountain?" Olga pointed to one of the peaks surrounding the lake. "The legend goes that a giant who lived in this lake reached out and grabbed at the top of the mountain, and that's how those indentations were formed." She walked over to the wall and rubbed her hands along a six-foot by eight-foot textile wall hanging. "They don't make these up here anymore. I've seen a few around Cuenca, though. Maybe they'll carry it on."

Back on the road we detoured into village after village, depressing in their squalor. "You see underdevelopment so often here," Olga said, "and so much of it, that after a while you don't see it anymore." We drove farther, and noticed the name Lenin on a few posters. "People called their children by names they saw in the newspapers and heard on the radio. They didn't know what they stood for. Names like Lenin and Adolph are not uncommon," Olga explained.

"Quechua names are almost always two syllables. I met an Indian couple once, and their little *guagua*," their baby, "was named Washco. 'What a pretty Quechua name!' I said. It turned out it was short for Washington. I repeated for Olga a story I'd heard about the police in Quito who once found a dead body on Jorge Washington Street. When they got to filling out the report, one cop asked the other, "How do you spell Washington?" "I don't know," his partner replied. "Let's move the body to Loja Street."

"This part of the Pana was paved about twenty years ago. All the Indians were so excited about it. They had never seen such a big, flat surface to lie down on, and at the opening they were all sprawled out drunk on the highway. I came up for the inauguration with Rolf Blomberg. We had to pull a few of them off the road like cadavers. Everyone had such a good time."

Finally, about five miles north of Otavalo, on a dirt road in the soft, hilly countryside, we arrived at the town of Peguche. "I think this is the house I want. No—pull up to that one over there. Wait. I'll ask these boys." Four youths walked by in homemade costumes, obviously on their way to some festivities. "Yes. Park in front of that pickup." Set back from the road was a ramshackle house. We walked through a doorway into a courtyard and up some rickety steps. The sounds of a wooden flute wafted from a room, and soon we were surrounded by an extended family of fifteen Otavalan Indians who greeted Doña Olga as one of their own.

Of sturdy build and aristocratic bearing, the Otavalans are known worldwide for the intricacy of their weavings and the expanse of their marketing. The men's long black braided hair and calf-length cotton pants, and the women's heavily beaded necklaces and colorful blouses, are seen in major cities the world over as they sell goods woven in Imbabura Province. Schooled in universities overseas, many Otavalans have escaped the bonds that shackle other Andean Indians.

Olga's friends were celebrating El Día de San Juan in their own home. Men lounged around the living room reading the morning paper from Quito. Women entered with bowls of *chicha*. A cassette deck played music by an internationally known local group, Nanda Mañanchi. One fellow strummed a guitar with a decal of Che tattooed on its shell. Another wailed on his bamboo flute, and a third accompanied the others on his harmonica. A shrine to Jesus, surrounded by candles dripping wax onto the floor, held a prominent spot. A collection basket rested in front of it. A dozen of the Indians danced to the music, single file, around and around. Quiet at first, their feet became the rhythm section, growing in volume until they stomped so hard the house fairly shook. The tune sounded like an endless repetition of the third line of "Frère Jacques." Some of them chanted in Quechua while their brethren paused for more *chicha*. Another donned a gorilla mask and kept running up to Olga in mock attack, squealing at her in a high-pitched voice. She feigned fear and everyone laughed. The noise became deafening. One of the stompers came over and urged Olga and me to join them. Normally slow of step and dependent upon a cane to steady herself, when invited to dance at a spirited Indian *fiesta* the octogenarian sprang alive. Her cane, which she pounded in rhythm with the beat, added to the floor's tremors as she kept pace with the dancers. More booze flowed. A boy of sixteen sat slumped on the couch, his eyes half-closed. "He's sleeping off this morning's drunk," Olga said through the din, "and resting up for the afternoon drink. He'll be fine."

Ten minutes later we were back outside in the pastoral countryside ready to leave when Julián Muenala, whose house we had just visited, walked up. "Give me a kiss," Olga exclaimed on seeing him. He and Olga, friends for thirty-five years, embraced. Behind his Oscar de la Renta sunglasses his eyes sparkled as he described his most recent trip to Italy. His business, selling Otavalan weavings, had originally been nurtured by Olga until it took wings of its own.

"The Otavalans are starting to use automated looms," Olga said as we headed back toward Quito. "They can make a lot more weavings in a shorter period of time, but they aren't as artistic as many of the other Indians. These are a highly cultured people, technically skilled and extremely smart. But they are not creative or original. I used to give them designs to weave. I don't do that anymore. They must do that on their own."

CHAPTER TWENTY-EIGHT

SOUR LAKE OIL

Most of Ecuador's Indians live in the central highlands between the two parallel mountain chains that make up the Andes. These are the indigenous people at the bottom of the social heap who plant corn, harvest potatoes, work for the better off—and make hats. Virtually all the rest of the Indians live in the Oriente, Ecuador's sparsely populated Amazon jungle region. Although geologists had spent decades drilling Indian hunting land for oil, not until the 1960s did they discover the country's future. Aboriginal Indians versus petrodollars—the face-off was too tempting to resist. The countdown for my Panama hat shipment to New York still allowed time for me to travel to the jungle for a look at the changes oil has brought about. Claude Levi Strauss's observation about South America rang true: "A continent barely touched by man," he wrote in *Tristes Tropiques*, "lay exposed to men whose greed could no longer be satisfied by their own continent."

What must the Indians have thought when the first Anglos came to their land? An Amazon-basin legend retold by Will Baker in *Backward* offers a clue: "It is said white men come to the *selva* with their gifts in order to capture the Indians, take them to secret places, and render them into oil which is used to power airplanes, motor boats and autos. So fueled, these craft return, bearing more gifts, seeking more Indians."

Some Indians refer to oil as "the black water that burns"; others call it "the excrement of the devil." By any name it has irrevocably altered the country since the first black gold was sent through the trans-Ecuadoran pipeline to the coast and shipped abroad in 1974. Nowhere had this change been more graphic than at Lago Agrio, Sour Lake in English, whose name comes not from any nearby body of rancid water but rather from Sour Lake, Texas, where a young company named Texaco had its first gusher in 1902. Carved from an unpopulated riverside rain forest, Lago Agrio has become a frontier jungle town that serves as a trading center for the Cofán Indians and as field headquarters for Texaco, Inc.

After a severe drought in the early 1970s struck Loja, hundreds of its residents were shuffled off to this new settlement on the Aguarico River. To encourage colonization, the government exempted new businesses from taxes and deeded land to homesteaders who kept crops in production. Some of the land had been traditional hunting territory for the Cofán and other Indians. Because Lago Agrio is only a short distance from Colombia, thousands of the ambitious, shiftless, and desperate from that country as well as Ecuador moved there for its remoteness and its frontier-style laxity.

Lago Agrio's airstrip has two terminals, one for the thrice-weekly commercial flight from Quito, and the other to serve the consortium between Texaco and the Corporación Estatal Petrolera Ecuatoriana (CEPE)—the Ecuadoran State Petroleum Corporation. When I visited, the main street of town was equal parts mud, oil, gravel, and tar, all sloshed together. Anything smaller than a pickup truck was doomed, especially during or after the daily torrential rainfall. Although Lago Agrio was no more than fifteen years old, it looked a weary fifty years old. Huge trucks from United States heavy-equipment companies rumbled through on their way to and from the fenced-in Texaco compound at the edge of town and the oil wells beyond. Bars, cafés, and bakeries competed for Ecuadoran *sucres* and Colombian *pesos*, available on the very public black market. Stores selling hardware, clothes, and music lined Lago's few streets. Chickens plucked coffee and cacao beans drying by the side of the road. Lanky Colombians, black and bony, played checkers in front of a Chinese restaurant while *cumbias* blasted from their cassette players. Most wore bathing suits or rolled-up pants, their feet covered by sandals or nothing. Machetes slapped against their thighs. Walking the streets of Lago Agrio for a few hours revealed a town with more sewing machines than toilets, more whorehouses than schoolhouses.

Down one street stood the Salón Descanso Intelectual, the Intellectual Resting Place, a small *cantina* whose sign pictured a man sitting at a school desk reading a book. Below an outdated wall calendar and a picture of a couple making love sat a phonograph on which the owner played both sides of a record—"Evil Thoughts" and "Heartless Woman." Afterward he carefully wiped it off with his hand, leaving mosquitoes and beads of sweat in its grooves. The Hollywood Beauty Salon was nearby. A couple of churches seemed planted only as an afterthought. On one, a poster quoted a smiling Pope John Paul II: "The well-being of the workers is more important than economic benefits."

The two most recommended hotels were the severely misnamed Residencia Hilton and the Residencia Utopia. "You'll like either one," a shop owner assured me. "Both use mosquito netting." A new one, El Cofán, was under construction, its restaurant already open for business. "For a while everyone called the town Nueva Loja because the first settlers were from Loja," its owner said. "The patron saint of Loja is the patron saint here. It's like our birthplace. We have had a violent struggle to establish a town—to get water, light, sewers, and electricity. Whatever we have in services here is inefficient and insufficient. Most people get their water from either the river or the rain. They promised us a lot, but gave us nothing."

The Vaquero Bar in the center of town had genuine Old West swinging doors in front and a laid-off oil-hand at the bar. On the stereo, Alexandra, the morning-shift bartender, played "Lost and Drunk" and "I'm a Vagabond" in honor of a customer who was all three. He told her about his twenty-two-year-old wife: "I ran her off. She was no good." He looked up at me. "I'm half-Cherokee and half-Irish. I grew up in Oklahoma." The words came out so slurred I couldn't tell which was worse, his Spanish or his English. "I been here six months. Have a beer? What's the matter, don't you like my railroad overalls?" He described each of his eight children and a six-pack of wives. Alexandra passed the time carefully cutting paper napkins in half with a scissors, doubling the Vaquero's supply. "Leaving so soon?" the jungle Okie asked. "Here." He leaned over and slobbered a loud kiss on me.

One fifth of all the women in Lago, which had ten thousand residents, were prostitutes, a doctor told me. "On the first Wednesday of every month we give them a checkup and a shot." Club Boricua, the current favorite, had oil-company trucks parked in the mud outside and wall paintings of couples in action inside. On oil-camp paydays, the place is jammed far into the night. Prostitutes sidle up for money for the Wurlitzer (one *sucre* for a song) or for themselves (five dollars for twenty minutes). Lago's finest brothel covers its jukebox with wire mesh to protect it from flying bottles and chairs.

"*El Oriente*," Henri Michaux wrote, "an Ecuadoran says this word as if it were *Paris*, both dangerous, hard to reach, and presumably awe-inspiring." When Claude Phillips first went there in the mid-1960s, it was all that and more. Phillips grew up in a poor southeast Texas farming family and worked on nearby oil rigs. "When I got here, there were no roads in this part of the Oriente, and only one well. They had to fly the entire rig over from Colombia. The town of Lago Agrio didn't exist. It was all jungle. We'd come down on rope ladders and clear the location with machetes and axes. We built a helicopter pad so choppers could come in. We had to bring a lot of equipment in on barges on the Aguarico River. It took us three months to build that airstrip. I was a maintenance foreman, but at the time there was nothing to maintain."

"Back then Ecuadoran workers got seven *sucres* a day plus sugar and water. They lived in a tent and had to hunt their own meat and bake their own bread—of course, there was nothing for them to make bread out of. We had both Indians and *mestizos*, anyone they'd throw into the jungle to work. I was criticized for even talking with Indians and others in the lower class. None of the workers even knew how to use a pipe wrench. In order to work with these people I couldn't be Claude, I had to be Claudio. So I changed my name. It worked."

Phillips and the others built a little thatch-roofed club. "We stocked cold beer. All we did was play cards. We had no women out there. I used to wander through the jungle by myself. I only got lost once." Phillips estimates that he has drilled more than three hundred oil wells in the Oriente over the years. "On the last one we drilled ninety-two hundred feet in eleven days and two hours. I was on the rig."

During his three-week breaks after twenty-one straight days on duty in the jungle, Phillips lives on a dollar salary in a *sucre* economy. With his Ecuadoran wife he has a large pinewood home in a valley outside Quito. Its shelves hold books by Steinbeck and Freud, videotapes of ballets, and recordings of Vivaldi and Bach. With prodding, his two parrots squawk "¡Por favor! ¡Por favor!" He goes deep-sea fishing off the coast and freshwater fishing on jungle rivers. Upper-class Ecuadoran friends join him for a round of golf on a local course, or at the house for a barbecue.

In the middle of one conversation he paused: "What's the word I want? My English is getting rusty. I don't use it too much anymore. I'm virtually an Ecuadoran citizen now. I've got a resident visa." He thought long and hard when I asked about the difficulties of the expatriate life. Finally he shook his head. "There are none for me. The younger ex-pats, though, they've never had a maid or a cook in their lives, then they come here and everything they want is provided for them. They can't adjust, especially the wives. For them it gets to the point where all they do is gripe."

The Texaco compound, a twenty-minute walk from the heart of town, is worlds apart from Lago Agrio. Past the armed guard are dormitories for the workers, company offices, a mess hall, machine shops, and storage sheds. Permanent subcontractors maintain huge facilities nearby. Their crews eat at Texaco's dining room and relax at the new two-million-dollar recreation building. The compound has its own electricity, hot water, and sewage facilities. Its lawns are manicured and its road paved. While Lago Agrio itself has few telephones, and most of them don't work, dormitories at the compound have phones in each room from which workers can talk toll-free with their families in Quito. In many ways Texaco's installation is like a little military base in a foreign country.

Since the CEPE-Texaco consortium's operations swung into full gear during the 1970s, more and more Ecuadorans, trained at their own universities, on the job, and in the States, have taken on office and field work. Most Texaco oilhands, in fact, are Ecuadoran—engineers, mechanics, technicians, and laborers. Like the gringos, they live in the cinder-block dorms, eat hearty company meals, and take the half-hour flight on the company jet back to their families in Quito for a long weekend.

The new recreation hall has brought Western civilization to the Amazon basin. Its bar looks like a happy-hour tavern, its movie theater shows Hollywood thrillers, and new pool tables and pinball machines bridge the time between games on the six automated bowling alleys. A wall-sized screen dominates the television room, and, for the more literary minded, a library offers books by Charles Dickens, Erskine Caldwell, and Richard Nixon. After years of makeshift entertainment, Texaco's oil-camp workers finally had a full-fledged modern student union. For the residents of Lago Agrio, it is off limits.

A planeload of government ministers, provincial mucky-mucks, and dignitaries from Quito and Texaco's Latin American headquarters in Florida flew in for the recreation hall's opening festivities. Bands played, booze flowed, visitors oohed and ahhed. Workers jammed the theater for the Miss CEPE-Texaco competition. Each of the six finalists was asked why she thought the Oriente should be developed. From Cristina Reynosa, the winning answer: "For the good of the country!" "¡Que Viva!" the crowd cheered. "¡Que Viva!"

Bill Allen, a professional bowler from Orlando, Florida, sat bewildered. "I was watching television at home a couple of days ago when I got a call from Brunswick asking if I'd make an appearance at the dedication of some new alleys. Now I'm in the Amazon jungle. Is it true that most of these people here have never even seen bowling?"

Claudio, who dropped in for the opening, nodded. "When you teach them something, you've got to be patient. Explain it very carefully over and over and look them in the eye. When they first say they understand, they usually don't. When that spark lights up in their eyes, they've learned. They'll do it right every time after that."

One hundred fifty Ecuadorans crowded in to watch their first game of bowling. Allen spoke over the public-address system: "Now you take four steps. If you're right-handed, start with your right foot. It's the rhythm, not the speed of the ball." Two Ecuadorans, encouraged by friends and alcohol, volunteered. Tossing gutter balls at first, they finally knocked down pins frame after frame, much to the delight of the spectators. In the next room, a visitor played "If I Were a Rich Man" on the saxophone.

"It's the beginning of the end," said Terry Andrews, who headed the workers association, as he marveled at the spanking new facilities. Andrews sat with David Archer, whose wife had just bowled the jungle's first strike. Archer, then Texaco's field-operations superintendent, agreed: "I never thought I'd see the day when we had bowling here. Ecuador was in a fifteenth-century economy before this," he added, indicating the promise of petroleum. "Now it's up to the nineteenth century."

Oil production in Ecuador has reached more than 275,000 barrels a day, most of which is shipped overseas. The income from that accounts for two-thirds of the country's total export earnings. "We figure it costs eighteen days a year to cover production costs, taxation, royalties, and concession fees," Archer said. "Texaco profit comes to one full day's production a year. The rest goes to the government. Our contract expires in 1992."

René Bucaram table-hopped around the opening-night party. Bucaram, from a Lebanese family long active in the country's affairs, ran all of Texaco's activities in Ecuador. Smooth and aggressive, he was its spokesman, liaison between the central government and corporate headquarters, and general top dog. "You work for me?" he said to Bernardo, a pipeline worker from Riobamba sitting at a table of celebrants.

"Yes, I work for you. But my interest is with Ecuador."

"Yeah? So is mine."

"What do you think of yourself?" Bernardo asked his top boss.

"I tell you, I'm a sonuvabitch. *Punto*. When I dropped down on that cable from a helicopter in 1970, there was nothing here. Nothing. I'm proud of that and all we've done out here since then. Everything else is just bullshit."

The boss drifted away, and Bernardo looked around at the party. "These people aren't Ecuadoran anymore. They've been corrupted. They know that technology equals dollars. You know what progress makes men? It makes them machines."

"I'll tell you what's wrong with development here," added Vince, who ran the electrical generator. "It's the Spanish influence. At the all-Ecuadoran operations nothing gets done. They're inefficient and there's corruption through and through."

Another worker complained about the brother of a top government official. "That guy requisitioned a tractor for two million *sucres*, then changed the purchase order to two million dollars. He paid for it and pocketed the rest. We call it 'the golden tractor.'"

"This is a boom town. The government takes money out, but they don't put it back in."

"Where do they put it?"

"Why, in their pockets!"

Someone told the story of a series of meetings between the oil ministers of Venezuela, Mexico, and Ecuador. As the three dined at an elegant ranch outside Caracas, the Venezuelan host motioned toward the road just beyond the estate's boundary. "You see that highway?" he exclaimed with pride. "We budgeted millions of *bolivares* for that. His guests nodded. "Ten percent," the Venezuelan said smugly, tapping his wallet. "Ten percent."

A few months later the three were again enjoying a leisurely business luncheon, this time on the veranda of an estate south of Mexico City. "Remember the airport you landed at yesterday?" the Mexican prompted his companions. "We just completed a five-year improvement plan out there, worth hundreds of millions of *pesos*." The two others complimented their host on a job well done. "Twenty percent," the Mexican confided, caressing his wallet. "Twenty percent."

The three oil chiefs met again early the next year on the patio of an old hacienda north of Quito. "You see that hydroelectric dam?" the Ecuadoran host asked of his friends as he motioned with an expansive sweep to the west. "It cost us half a billion *sucres*." The Venezuelan and the Mexican squinted hard, searching the landscape in vain for the dam. "A hundred percent," said the smiling Ecuadoran, patting his wallet. "A hundred percent."

BIENVENIDO—HOUSTON, ECUADOR. That's what the roadside welcome sign said as our chartered bus approached Shushufindi, an oil camp much farther out in the jungle. The trees, vines, and underbrush in the equatorial rain forest wore an astounding variety of greens: dark green, black green, light green, blinding green, thick green, young green, floor green, lively green, and forever green. Trees grow up so fast that they don't have a chance to grow wide. A path cleared by machete is gone within a week.

To get to the bus we crossed the Aguarico River in a motorboat during a storm, just missing logs bounding downriver. With me in the wind-tossed boat were salesmen for oil-field-equipment manufacturers, the United States Embassy Commercial Attaché, and other guests on their way to a birthday party for Minga, a company that sells and services oil-field equipment. The road to Shushufindi parallels the pipeline, which was covered with political graffiti and draped with drying laundry from homes in the few settlements along the way.

Local residents have to step over the pipeline to reach the road every day. Their horses and mules do likewise. More than a hundred people came to wish Minga a happy birthday in a huge jungle warehouse that served as the company's field headquarters.

Outside, a soccer game was just finishing up. Inside, Western swing music alternated with Ecuadoran pop; rock 'n' roll with salsa. Workers from Minga, Texaco, and its subcontractors danced with teachers from area schools and others from Lago Agrio and Quito. One Texaco oil-hand wanted to talk about working for a multinational corporation: "During the oil glut a few years ago we'd work twenty-eight days. No one bitched when they told us we had to move our residence to Ecuador. I'm a bachelor and I've got a four-bedroom place in the Mariscal Sucre area in Quito. Company-housing allowance pays for my apartment. We've got profit-sharing—for every dollar I put in, they match it. We're considered full-time residents here. The company pays our Ecuadoran taxes; since we're ex-pats, we don't have to pay U.S. taxes. The married workers send their kids to private schools in Quito and get home leave for the whole family." He left to flirt with a local schoolteacher. They danced two numbers. The Latin one I couldn't follow, but this much I know to be true: Amazon jungle Indians dance a lousy Cotton-Eyed Joe.

Around the bar, men talked about the Dallas Cowboys, Minnesota Fats, and the pretty lady sitting by herself at a nearby table. This was the jet-set petroleum crowd, gossiping about its calling: "We're down here on a swing through Ecuador on our way to Colombia. We just finished drilling in Peru." "I'd move to Quito in a heartbeat, unless I could move to Midland. I'd play golf every morning," said the representative from TRW Corporation. "I woke up in Tulsa yesterday, took a flight to Dallas and over to Miami, then down here." "Britt's going to talk with Occidental about landing their contract. We'd like to establish oil-field networks all over South America." "Where's that place in Caracas you stayed at last month?" I left around one in the morning. The bartender and the phonograph worked on into the steamy night.

CHAPTER TWENTY-NINE

TO COLOMBIA

Ildefonso Muñoz insisted I visit Colombia, his homeland. Muñoz, in his late fifties, came to Ecuador in 1950, either because he was a Protestant under a government that was intolerantly Catholic, or because he was on the losing side of a coup (the truth depends on which story you prefer). During his first two decades in Ecuador he owned and rented out a few bungalows on the Aguarico River west of present-day Lago Agrio at a place he named Muñozlandia. His tenants included ichthyologists from the United States, one of whom named a creature after him: *Centrolenella muñozorum*. A man who remembers Muñoz from the early days described him as a renegade: "He had been converted by the missionaries, and went out to convert others. The missionaries would drop charity supplies that said FRIENDSHIP FROM THE PEOPLE OF THE UNITED STATES; and he'd sell the stuff in his *tienda*. At the time Puyo was the biggest place in the jungle, and he'd strut into town with a six-shooter strapped to his hip and a cowboy hat on his head."

This particular afternoon Muñoz wore dirty jeans and a soiled yellow *guayabera* offset by his sparkling eyes, shining teeth under a black mustache, and slicked-back thinning hair. He stood behind the counter of his restaurant, Piragua, lettering a birthday sign for a party in honor of a CEPE-Texaco worker later that evening. His menagerie of jungle animals kept their distance outside: a thigh-thick boa constrictor, a giant rodent, and a *tigrillo*. At Halloween Muñoz hangs foot-and-a-half-long crocodiles from the ceiling. "They snap at people's ears. It's all in fun."

Muñoz had been in Lago Agrio from its beginning, and knew more about its people than anyone. His restaurant had a reputation for relative cleanliness and good food. On Thursday nights he serves *chile con carne* to the Texans who venture out of the compound for dinner. "One year the workers were going to take up a collection for me to go to the chili cook-off at Terlingua, Texas." The idea fell through, but Muñoz was honored at the thought.

"I want you to try a drink I have prepared. It's called *sinchicara*. Here. Have a shot." It was grape-colored, but so bitter that sucking a lemon afterward seemed sweet. The flavor was lost between the bite and the afterbite. "You like it? I make it myself from my own private formula. If you take it first thing in the morning, you don't even need breakfast. It'll give you enough energy for the entire day.

"*Sinchicara* has five ingredients. All of them grow here in the jungle." He named four of them. "The last one—that's my secret! I've patented it. It's good for arthritis and grippe, and it kills off amoebas. People swear by it." I asked for a second shot. "It's a sort of hallucinogen. It costs two dollars and fifty cents a bottle."

Fausto, a mechanic from the garage next door, nodded. "It gives you the strength of Samson."

"It takes three days to make, then fifteen days distilling. I've always got some brewing. Once I shipped a few bottles to some doctors in Chicago."

Just as the *sinchicara* started to take effect, a middle-aged Southern Baptist missionary couple walked in and sat down at the table next to me. "We've only been in the Oriente a few years," Elaine Joiner volunteered, "but we've lived in the country for thirty years. We started out here by setting up a sheet on a wall and sent a truck through town advertising movies with a religious theme. In Quito we had rocks and bottles thrown at us when we did that. Of course that was before Pope John.

"Our work is to help the Lord make a change in the people by teaching the word of God. There's a town of Secoya Indians where missionaries have been at work for twenty years. As a result, most of the Indians there are now Christians. Garreth here, he's sort of a circuit rider. He goes from Indian village to Indian village."

Garreth had a theory that the transistor radio was responsible for the acceptance of evangelists in the countryside: "The Indians and others were softened up by HCJB," the evangelical multilingual shortwave station from Quito. "When we got here they already knew what we were all about." The Joiners live in a prefab suburban home near the banks of the Aguarico. "There's a house of prostitution not far from us. Prostitution isn't supposed to take place within three kilometers of a school or a residence, but the Mafia runs prostitution here. There's so much money in it." Sr. Muñoz served me another *trago* of his psychedelic home brew.

Elaine, again: "It's a rewarding experience. There's always something new. We're appreciated. After thirty-three years we're still Americans. We like sliced bread and potato chips. But we realized during the strike that we were trapped." Earlier that year workers in the Oriente staged a general strike, closing down the one road to Quito and sabotaging oil production and the pipeline. It ended when the government promised to pour money into the region and provide more services.

Elaine answered slowly when I asked what she missed about the States. "I suppose what I miss most is American women to talk with. The idea of not having your own kind. We try to think we blend in with the foliage, but every now and then we are reminded that we are foreigners."

Garreth had an answer quicker than the question: "Spare parts. When something goes wrong with the car or we need a new bushwhacker, we have to wait a month or more."

After the Joiners left, Muñoz reflected on the influx of missionaries, oil companies, and homesteaders. "You know, civilization in this area is like feeding strong medicine for a small illness. It almost kills the patient. Sudden civilization has done that here. For example, the Cofán Indians were primitive people when the oil companies came. They were very sane. With the oil companies came civilization and liquor and *aguardiente*. They've changed a lot since then." I recalled a comment that David Archer, the Texaco supervisor, had made about the Cofán: "I used to get a string of beads from them for a cigarette. Now they think nothing of asking three hundred *sucres*."

Muñoz laid out an itinerary for me. I should visit Colombia one day, and the Indians the next. He'd find some Cofán in town to ride the bus with me out to Dureno, their village downriver.

The San Miguel River fifteen miles north of Lago Agrio separates Ecuador from Colombia. The port village there is San Miguel, but everyone calls it La Punta. An open-air bus painted like a circus poster left Lago every three hours. On my midmorning ride the driver kept constant pressure on the horn, which repeatedly squawked out the first ten notes of "La Marseillaise." He dropped us off at the dock, where soldiers from the military garrison checked to make sure we weren't guerrillas. We paid 250 Colombian *pesos* each for a forty-five-minute motorized canoe ride to Puerto Colón on the Colombian side of the river. Three of the other eight passengers were cows, strapped down in the middle of the canoe.

The jungle looked the same on both banks—dense, high, and impenetrable. On the Colombian side a small hut appeared every few minutes, its occupants waving lackadaisically. The sun shone brilliantly through a clear equatorial sky. The Amazon jungle was at its friendliest. My fellow passengers were locals attuned to the customs of both sides. They traded in cattle, crops, and small merchandise, back and forth every day.

At Ipiales, Colombia's major border town with Ecuador on the Pan-American Highway, the National Police welcome visitors with a full-page warning:

- Don't leave your car unattended when you go to make purchases.

- Guard your personal possessions.

- Avoid transactions with strangers or suspicious people.

- Don't display any money or jewelry on the sidewalk.

- When you go to deposit or withdraw money from the bank, ask a policeman to accompany you.

As we got closer to Puerto Colón, a friend's warning came to mind: "You watch yourself when you go to Colombia. They'll steal the milk right out of your coffee."

When we docked, the six of us got out of the canoe and scrambled up a hill to pass immigration. The border official, a soldier a few sizes smaller than his uniform, perfunctorily nodded the first three men through, then looked up at me. "Papers, please," he said without emotion. I slid my passport out of its waterproof case and handed it to him. (Border-crossing tip: In delicate situations, always proffer your passport as if surrendering a weapon—handle-side toward your opposite.) "I'm only planning to stay in Colombia for the afternoon," I told him, "then catch the late canoe back to Ecuador." He looked at my passport photo, then up at me, then back to the picture, then up to my chin.

"I shaved."

"Do you have any other documents?" His voice was unarmed. I rummaged through my shoulder bag—pen and notebook, newspaper clippings, a jacket, the University of Chicago pocket Spanish-English dictionary, *Nostromo* by Joseph Conrad, and a map—and finally came up with a wrinkled photocopy of a letter of introduction from my editor in New York. I handed it to him and held my breath as he slowly moved his lips through the florid Spanish courtesies: "*Les agradeceremos de antemano las cortesías y la cooperación que le proporcionen . . .*" The Colombian border guard nodded and bowed slightly. "*Pásale,*" he said solemnly. You may enter.

So different! With just a river to separate the two countries, the people of Puerto Colón had a personality distinct from Ecuadorans. They carried themselves more rhythmically and with more confidence. They were looser, smoother talking, and quicker to smile. The town itself was a pitiful little river port, small enough to be walked in half an hour, relaxed enough to find people to chat with everywhere. Morning fishermen hauled in their daily catch. Soldiers from the local military camp kicked a soccer ball around. Mothers swept their porches and chased their children. A bus sputtered down the main street, about to embark for quieter towns in the interior. Daytime prostitutes waved from dockside hovels. Most men wore wide-brimmed hats whose straw was coarser and sturdier than *paja toquilla* and whose designs involved intricate black interweavings. The men and women of Puerto Colón showed a measure of prosperity slightly higher than that in La Punta downriver.

One reason may be overflow from some of the world's most productive coca cultivation and processing operations nearby. In one 1984 drug raid northeast of Puerto Colón, for example, almost fourteen tons of cocaine were discovered—the largest seizure at any one time anywhere. Because of its enormous cocaine traffic, Colombia may be the only country where the black-market dollar is actually worth less than the official exchange rate.

Ecuadoran police and the U.S. Drug Enforcement Administration have flown helicopters over and motored down the same stretch of the San Miguel River that I traveled, finding coca fields just a few hundred yards south of the river. Hidden near the fields were laboratories for processing the leaves into paste. The discovery raised Ecuador's status from a country through which coca was merely transported to one estimated by the U.S. State Department as possibly the world's third largest coca producer. Some coca farmers, who live in crude thatched jungle huts, have satellite dishes hooked up to color televisions powered by gas generators. Commenting about the drug farmers near the San Miguel River, an investigator reported that "one can be a hundred miles from the nearest road or village and find Indians watching MTV." The sleepy stretch of the San Miguel between the two countries, so friendly and easy to travel, turned out to be one of South America's major drug highways.

CHAPTER THIRTY

UP THE AGUARICO

The next day I took a wood-frame bus from Lago Agrio to Dureno. Watercolor drawings covered its side, and cases of Coca-Cola destined for settlements deep in the jungle bounced on top. A sign on the back said DON'T BOTHER ME—I'M CRAZY. Some thirty passengers had boarded by the time the bus completed its swing through town— elderly fair-skinned men with bedrolls and straw hats, and thin black women in loose print dresses with children under their arms. Some carried umbrellas to protect themselves from the sun. Sr. Muñoz had arranged for Mauricio and his son Luis, two Cofán Indians who had been in town selling beaded necklaces and lances to tourist shops, to take me to Dureno. There I might find Randy, a gringo born and raised by missionary parents. The lances the two Cofáns sold were unlike the longer ones their tribe used to make, but the shorter ones sold well, and better still if they were adorned with feathers. Likewise, the more color they put in their necklaces, the more they sold. Mauricio was dressed in a loose shirt which hung to his knees over baggy, rolled-up corduroy pants. He went barefoot. No more than fifty whiskers protruded from his handsome oval face. His front teeth looked as though they had been absorbed by his gums. His headband appeared to be a corn husk. Luis dressed in bell-bottoms, sandals, and a T-shirt. The two talked in the tribal tongue spoken by all three hundred Cofáns.

Mauricio turned to me. "Do you have your documents with you? The military checkpoint is just ahead." We sat next to each other and talked some, but the engine's noise and our distance made for a strained conversation. The pipeline road we traveled on had been built during the previous decade. Huge equipment trucks roared up and down it every hour. For part of the trip we could see the Aguarico, which flowed on our right. Thick brush grew all around, including a vine so strong it choked full-grown trees to death and became a tree itself. After an hour Mauricio signaled the driver to stop. "This is it. Let's get off here."

There was nothing to distinguish the spot from any other. The jungle looked just as thick and the area just as desolate as anything we had seen for most of the ride. Luis pulled some brush to the side, uncovering a wide path leading downhill toward the Aguarico. Just before we reached the river he moved some more brush aside and pulled out a paddle and a long bamboo pole. The family canoe was parked at the end of the path. We hopped into the thirty-foot craft, Mauricio in front with the pole, Luis in the rear with the paddle, and the fearful white tourist crouched in the middle. How symbolic, I thought, to have these two Indians doing all the work while the visiting gringo simply sits in the middle. Why, this was how the West was won! And in Ecuador, the East too. Mauricio jarred me out of this disturbing realization when, about halfway across the river, he turned and said: "Oh, by the way, this will cost twenty *sucres*."

About a half mile downriver we drifted up to a sandbar, and the two of them got out to push and pull the boat to its parking spot on the Dureno side of the river. We waded knee-deep across a small inlet, and Mauricio led me up a steep hill and onto a jungle path from which we could hear laughing voices coming from the village. The Cofán language, full of false starts and glottal stops, had been written and preserved by missionaries from the controversial Summer Institute of Linguistics. The only familiar word was gringo, which often as not was followed by laughter. We walked across a soccer field that had been a landing strip for the missionaries until they were formally evicted in 1981. At the end of the soccer field was a combination schoolhouse and auditorium. The houses, open-air thatched-roof homes with almost no furniture, were built on sturdy hardwood posts. Mauricio's cousin and her five children joined us as we paraded past the last of the houses down a path to Randy's place. He had gone out for a while, Mauricio learned. He would be back shortly.

Randy's home, still under construction, looked like its blueprint had come from *Sunset Magazine*. Two-by-fours, crossbeams, a doorway, two stories—this was the Taj Mahal of Dureno. A generator nearby powered a community freezer.

Hesitant to move about too freely, I waited in a chair. As the sun sank deeper, strange sounds grew louder. Full-throated bird trills rolled through the trees. Invisible animals raced through the underbrush, leaving sudden noises hanging in the sticky air. A series of croaks in what seemed like three-part harmony punctuated the stillness. Loud mosquitoes gathered around me. Bamboo whistles played in the village. I pulled out my pocket dictionary to look up some nagging verb tenses, although from what I'd been told, these people didn't have much of a future—their lives were strictly present tense, and conditional at that.

Footsteps approached on the path from the village and a short, muscular Indian walked straight at me. He wore a feather through his nose and carried a rifle and a machete. Though apparently confronting an Amazon savage armed to the teeth, I sensed no danger whatsoever, and in fact found the man rather friendly. He was a tribal elder, and the feather, merely decorative. Oh yes, he said. Randy should be back soon. Feathernose walked off to hunt his dinner.

Long after nightfall Randy appeared, alerted by others that a stranger waited at his home. In his twenties, my host looked like the all-American boy. By circumstance and preference, however, he was more Cofán than anything else. He had tried attending college in the States, but soon realized his life back in the Amazon made more sense. So he eats, hunts, and plays with his fellow Indians, acting as a missionary without portfolio. Guiding river expeditions for adventure travel groups from the States brings in a healthy income for himself and the tribe.

Randy maneuvered around his unfinished cabin by swinging from pole to pole, first down to the ground floor, then up and around to his sleeping loft. "Hold on, I'll be right back," he said as he walked out with a twenty-gauge shotgun. A couple of minutes later one shot went off. He returned clutching a boat-billed heron. "There. This bird will be put in tomorrow's stew. It'll feed my family." A family of eight shared meals with their gringo.

Randy disparaged Lago Agrio and the oil camps. "When Lago had six houses, five of them served alcohol and three of those had whores. Texaco's just asking for trouble. The contrast is becoming so great. The only reason they've been able to get away with it so far is that they employ so many Ecuadorans.

"Out here we live mainly by hunting and fishing. We do a little lumbering too. Before the pipeline road was built it took us a day to get to Lago by canoe. When we began to put motors on them we cut our time to two and a half hours. We've tried to make the most of the road without letting it affect us too much. Before, our hunting lands were much larger. Now we have ninety-five hundred hectares, all on this side of the Aguarico. I'll show you some of the territory tomorrow."

"Sorry," Randy said the next morning, after a breakfast of pulped and boiled yucca with his family. "I've got to go out on a drug bust." He and a dozen other Cofáns, including Feathernose, armed themselves with rifles, machetes, and a blowgun. "We've heard that a few of our people who live outside the village are growing marijuana and coca leaves as a cash crop. If they're caught, they could lose it for the rest of us. I'd like to take you, but I'm not sure what's going to happen. See that house over there? Ask for Arturo. He'll take you back across the river."

Arturo wasn't home and the narcs had already left, so I wandered around the village hoping to find someone else going across the river. One man led me to another and another and another, until finally Eduardo agreed to take me across in his motorized canoe with his family of eight.

The previous morning I had been checking my map. The Aguarico fed into the Napo, and the Napo flowed all the way down to the Amazon, which eventually emptied into the Atlantic Ocean. Roughly figured, the whole trip would cover a thousand miles. At forty miles a day we'd reach the Atlantic within a month. Eduardo sensibly ignored my entreaty.

One of the innumerable problems we would have encountered along the way would have been nationality. Ecuador's claim over the western Amazon basin, now recognized by virtually every other country as belonging to Peru, ranks among Latin America's most longstanding unresolved border problems. The two nations have historically been at odds with each other over where the line between them lies. At both the bargaining table and on the battlefield, Peru has almost always walked away the winner. Ecuador's contention has become a source of frustration and nationalism and has led to minor but regular skirmishes along the border. Between 1978 and 1984 the two countries clashed five times at remote outposts; the boundary remained intact.

The conflict goes back to the conquistadors, when Gonzalo Pizarro in Quito, acting on behalf of his big brother Francisco in Cuzco, sent Francisco de Orellana out to look for a lost detachment in the jungle-land east of the Andes. Orellana never located the missing soldiers, but he did find the waterways intriguing, and instead of reporting back to his boss, he pressed eastward. Six months later, in 1542, he floated out the mouth of the Amazon and sailed on to Spain, where he was named governor of the Amazon region as a reward. Twenty-one years later King Philip II put the Amazon territory in Quito's domain.

Over the years Peru has nibbled away at Ecuador, once even occupying Guayaquil. In 1941 its military superiority overran Ecuador's profoundly underequipped army and claimed most of Ecuador's land east of the Andes. (The U.S. Consul General in Guayaquil asked Washington for "two tear gas guns in the event of disorder to be expected if Peru should occupy Guayaquil.") Humiliated, Ecuador limped to Rio de Janeiro, and at the urging of "disinterested third parties"—Argentina, Brazil, Chile, and the United States—signed away the disputed territory. The treaty, signed in 1942, was called the Protocol of Peace, Friendship, and Limits, although it was none of those. By taking the land away, Peru effectively denied Ecuador access to the Marañón River, hence a direct route to the Amazon River and the Atlantic Ocean.

Ecuador never really accepted the protocol, insisting that it had signed the treaty with a gun to its head. In 1960 Ecuador's President Velasco Ibarra unilaterally declared the eighteen-year-old treaty null and void. Ecuador maintains, at least cartographically, the notion that Iquitos, that most Peruvian jungle outpost, is part of Ecuador. A dotted line on Ecuadoran maps begrudgingly acknowledges the reality of Peru's land grab, and even then it insists that about forty-five miles of the 1942 border is impossible to ascertain. All maps published in Ecuador must show the country in its pre-1942 bulge, rather than as the rest of the world sees it.

In Peru the dispute fuels enmity. Mario Vargas Llosa, the Peruvian author, has written that when he mocked his country's military in his first novel, a general claimed that he had "undoubtedly been paid by

Ecuador to undermine the prestige of the Peruvian Army." Journalists in Peru unleashed venomous attacks upon a Mexican television personality when, during an international broadcast in 1984, he said that Ecuador was the birthplace of the Amazon. A "pro-Ecuadoran ignoramus," wrote one columnist.

The word *Amazon* is constantly bandied about Ecuador to boost morale over a cause that is irrevocably lost. Official government stationery proclaims: "Ecuador has been, is, and will be an Amazonian country." In Quito one day I was having lunch with an acquaintance when a friend of his showed up. She was introduced as the granddaughter of the president during the 1941 war with Peru and the subsequent treaty. "Oh!" I blurted out rather undiplomatically. "Your grandfather was the one who signed away half the country!" "Well, yes," she quickly admitted. "But if he hadn't, they'd have taken it all. We'd be in Peru right now, not Ecuador." Although Ecuador's claim is well taken, Peru won't give back the land it stole until the Amazon River dries up, and not before.*

---

* In October 1998 the two countries formally and finally signed a peace treaty resolving the border conflict—in Peru's favor.

CHAPTER THIRTY-ONE

MADELINE IN QUITO

"To the Europeans," said the doctor in Gabriel García Márquez's *No One Writes to the Colonel*, "South America's a man with a mustache, a guitar, and a gun." Such stereotypes are born of observation, superficial and redundant. By the time they get back to the observed, they are usually skewed, corny, and insulting. Seldom do people see themselves in the words of others. Ecuadorans were well-disposed toward my own task, but also wary. Too well do they remember Ludwig Bemelmans.

Bemelmans published forty-two books, best known among them his *Madeline* series for children. Illustrations by the Austrian-born New Yorker enhanced his writings. In Ecuador his name means foreigner-who-makes-fun-of-natives, all because of his 1941 book, *The Donkey Inside*. "'We have a revolution here every Thursday afternoon at half past two,'" Bemelmans quotes a native, "'and our government is run like a nightclub. We owe some two hundred and fifty million *sucres*; but who pays debts these days?'" About the food: "The cooks are not very good in Ecuador, but then you have two of them." Of fashion and beauty: "Of all the women here, perhaps a half dozen are beautiful and four of these dress with taste." With gloved jabs, Bemelmans mocked clerical pomposity, official hypocrisy, and anything else that struck him as ludicrous and comical. He was game for adventure, both high and low, and obviously enjoyed himself: "Quito is kind of a penal colony for diplomats. In some cases they are banished to this high capital for minor indiscretions, alcoholism, badly conducted affairs of the heart or the state. . . . This makes on the whole for a group of likeable, outspoken, and refreshing people. Not being *persona grata* with their own governments, they get along well with their hosts, tell well-flavored stories, and are usually excellent companions."

When his book was published the same year in Ecuador, *El Burro por Dentro* caused a sensation, denounced from the pulpit and the soapbox. It was sold under the counter. "Bemelmans ridiculed us in an amiable way, but few people understood," said author Nicolás Kingman when I met him at his bookstore. Kingman recalled that the intellectual class liked *Burro*. "It was authentic and realistic. You must understand we had many prejudices then. There was intense nationalism. It was the same year as the border war with Peru. We were very Catholic and the Church often intervened in daily life. The upper class was offended. In order to change things we needed something like Bemelmans's book." A commentator in Quito wrote at the time, "many Ecuadorans have had to dance the conga of pure indignation."

The literary scandal has not yet abated. Bemelmans is still seen in Ecuador as a twentieth-century Baron Munchausen, the legendary German who told tall tales of foreign adventures. More than four decades after *The Donkey Inside* was published, and more than twenty years since the author's death, a Quito bookseller told me, "I can stock Philip Agee's book about the CIA in Ecuador, but to carry *El Burro por Dentro* could be suicidal." In *El Comercio*, columnist Jorge Ribadeneira uses *Donkey* as a point of departure to write of changes during the intervening years.

For all his mockery, Bemelmans's warmth and affection for the land and its people burns through: "For those who still dream, the jungles, the seacoast, the tropic isles, and the mountains of Ecuador offer all the scenery, every variety of climate, and they are the ideal proving ground for adventure and escape. . . ." Virtually unknown to Ecuadorans, however, are two other books Bemelmans wrote about their country: for children, *Quito Express*, about a little Otavalan boy who rides the train to Guayaquil; and *Now I Lay Me Down to Sleep*, a novel about a general living in European exile who returns to his Ecuadoran *hacienda*. In the United States, Bemelmans's legacy can be seen at New York's Carlyle Hotel, where his artwork still covers the walls of the bar bearing his name.

I would feel more comfortable defending Bemelmans had I not learned of his anti-Semitic impulses from two people who met him back then. Benno Weiser Varon, then a newspaper columnist and a leader of Quito's Jewish community, remembered that Bemelmans urged the Quito Tennis Club to exclude Jews. Olga Fisch recollected that the author convinced expatriate photographer André Roosevelt, a distant cousin to Franklin, to start a club called La Cucaracha Alegre (The Happy Cockroach) and not admit Jews. The club, according to Olga, went broke within a week.

"You will write well about us, won't you?" Over and over the question was asked by people fiercely proud of their country yet understandably cautious. Travel literature is full of Ecuador seen mainly in terms of other countries: Salinas is "the Miami of Ecuador" and Cuenca "the Athens of Ecuador"; Esmeraldas has "African black richness"; there are "Tibetan-like herds at the base of Mt. Chimborazo"; and Cotopaxi is "the Fujiyama of Ecuador." Ecuadorans were naturally amazed to learn that the equation has once been reversed: In Colorado, there is a tiny town called Cotopaxi, named by a well-traveled miner who noticed a striking resemblance between a distant peak in the Rocky Mountains and the volcano south of Quito.

The loss of national identity is not limited to tourist literature or straw hats: The writer Ben Hecht contributed to Ecuador's image with his 1937 play *To Quito and Back*, about fervent revolution and unfulfilled dreams. "I mean nothing disrespectful toward Ecuador," Hecht's patronizing Britisher tells a naïve girl, "but you can't take a country seriously one of whose major political problems is a firm stand against head-hunting and cannibalism." At the 1984 Los Angeles Summer Olympics, ABC television anchorman Peter Jennings briefly praised each country as its standard-bearer entered the Memorial Coliseum. When Ecuador's yellow, blue, and red flag came on camera, Jennings found fourteen words: "The conquistadores stopped in Ecuador. They didn't find enough riches, so they moved on."

The best English-language books about Ecuadorans coping with life at the bottom are *Living Poor* and its companion, *The Farm on the River of Emeralds*, both by Moritz Thomsen. His accounts, moving and funny, tell of the wrenching frustrations and unexpected rewards that occur when the First World meets the Third. For three years a Peace Corps volunteer in Ecuador in the mid-1960s, Thomsen now lives—and writes—on a small farm near the Esmeraldas River. For a number of years he lived in Quito, where he could usually be found holding literary court at a neighborly seafood café. He is the only

English-language writer who has captured Ecuador from the inside looking out. He would agree, I am sure, with Robert Byron, who in *The Road to Oxiana* defends traveling writers whose books insult their hosts: "Somebody must trespass on the taboos of modern nationalism, in the interest of human reason. Business can't. Diplomacy won't. It has to be people like us."

To me, Ecuador had been a country with its head in the clouds, its heart on its sleeve, and its groin to the ground. Columnist Jorge Ribadeneira's reassuring words accompanied me as I prepared to leave the country: "Not everything is perfect, and there is still material for another *'pollino por dentro,'*" a little donkey inside.

CHAPTER THIRTY-TWO

CROSSING THE LINE

The hats from Cuenca had already arrived in New York, where they waited for Karl Dorfzaun to forward them on to Resistol in Texas. I was still in South America, having strayed too far from the trail. It was certainly time to return.

Few passenger-freighters dock on Ecuador's coast anymore, but one was due soon at Puerto Bolívar, south of Guayaquil. By taking it I would follow the old trade routes that bananas, coffee, cacao, and straw hats once took. In fact, except for the hats, the S.S. *Santa Maria* seemed to be still loading all these things. I climbed the steps to the main deck, tiptoed around the snoozing immigration officer who was to stamp my passport, and found my room. I was the only passenger who boarded in Ecuador.

The ship's five top decks housed and fed passengers; the four decks below carried freight. It measured 180 yards long and weighed 20,000 tons. Some eighty passengers were aboard, most of whom had begun their voyage in San Francisco or Los Angeles. Their eight-week cruise took them south to Colombia, through the Panama Canal, and along South America's east coast and through the Strait of Magellan. From there they called at Chile and Peru, and finally Puerto Bolívar, the *Santa Maria*'s last stop before returning to the United States. The average age of the passengers was seventy-three, down slightly due to the onboard death of an eighty-two-year-old man and my arrival.

We left early one morning, chugging northwest through the Gulf of Guayaquil. Later that day we were to cross the equator, the name adopted by the country I'd finally left. The ship's crew had prepared a "bottle message ceremony" for us and gave us each a parchment printed in English and Spanish: "If perchance, this bottle's found/Let me know where it went aground,/Just write to me without delay/I'll send a dollar . . . right away!!!" Below that was space for a name and address. We were to place the note inside an empty wine bottle, seal it, and then, when the ship's horn bleated, we were to toss them over the starboard side.

The bottle ceremony seemed perfectly silly. The equator itself, however, had fascinated me as far back as I could remember. When this book was taking form in my mind, I daydreamed about traveling along 0 degrees latitude all the way around the world. My trip would begin at the Galápagos Islands and proceed westward 24,000 miles until I returned to the equatorial monument just north of Quito. I spent most of two days poring over detailed topographic maps, each one covering a 350-mile stretch of the 25,000-mile equatorial circum-ference. In all, I would have traveled through almost fifty countries, including tiny island nations. To my dismay, I found that the equator passes through some of the most miserable parts of the world.

Although the nineteenth-century theory that tropical countries experience more turmoil than those in the temperate zones had been discarded, I envisioned enough trouble, political and health, to make me dismiss the equatorial route right away. There were further obstacles: In South America alone, fourteen languages are spoken on the line; the Congo and Uganda have unpronounceable towns whose names have four consonants in a row, and a river with four consecutive vowels flows through Gabon; Sumatra has a town with twenty-two letters: Bandjarsialanbertunggu. Lake Victoria and the Amazon River enticed me, but high-altitude ice climbing in Kenya did not. What intrigued—and repulsed—me most on the maps were entire regions marked "unexplored," "approximate," or the foreboding "abandoned." Following the equator was a trip I'd rather read about than take (and a book title Mark Twain had already used). And so I tossed my message bottle into the Pacific Ocean and watched it bob off into the distance.

Our bottle ceremony was tepid compared to the real tradition, one that has a long and somewhat honorable history among seafarers. One sailor dresses himself as King Neptune and subjects "polliwogs"— those who have never crossed the equator at sea—to playful humil-iation, such as a dunking, shaving, paddling, or recantation of public acts. When Charles Darwin crossed the equator aboard the *Beagle* in

1832, he and other initiates were blindfolded, drenched with buckets of water, and led upon a plank that tilted into a large bath. "They then lathered my face & mouth with pitch and paint," he wrote in his diary, "& scraped some of it off with a piece of roughened iron hoop." Survivors of the nautical hazing become "shellbacks."

Unlike 0 degrees longitude at Greenwich, England, an arbitrary international designation a mere century old, the equator goes back to the planet's creation. It forms the seam of the earth. "There isn't a Parallel of Latitude but thinks it would have been the Equator if it had had its rights," wrote Mark Twain, who reported his crossing thus: "A sailor explained to a young girl that the ship's speed is poor because we are climbing up a bulge toward the center of the globe; but that when we should once get over, at the Equator, and start down-hill, we should fly." Olga Fisch had said that when she was a child in Hungary, she thought the equator was a silver band and little girls had to shine it.

A few weeks before leaving Ecuador I received a letter from a friend who wrote while sitting at a bar in Kenya; half the bar was in the Southern Hemisphere and the other half was in the Northern. At the equator monument near Quito, tourists arrive by the busful to have their pictures taken standing astride the middle of the world.

Ecuador has become a leader in a most unusual international fray involving the ribbon around the earth 22,300 miles above the Equator. In effect, what Ecuador and other countries along the Equator say is, if a country controls the land beneath it and the water around it, why not the space above it? They want a voice in regulating the satellite space over their countries, rather like the Law of the Sea stood on its head. This novel approach to international law may be symbolic, but it provides Ecuador and the other countries with their only voice in the politics of outer space.

After I returned to the United States I went back out to follow the hats again as they crossed the North American continent. During my absence a letter arrived postmarked Quito. Five days after my ship left Ecuador, a thirteen-year-old boy happened to be walking along a deserted stretch of beach near Salinas, and a glimmer of light reflected off something rolling up out of the tide. What was it—a rock? A seashell? Andrés Barsky, whose family was vacationing from their home in Quito, took a close look. My bottle had drifted ashore.

Andrés's family lived in self-imposed exile from their native Argentina, waiting for the return of democracy to their homeland. His mother is a psychologist; his father, a sociologist studying rural Ecuador. Among the communities he had researched was one where *paja toquilla* grows.

Andrés and I became pen pals—he writing about his progress in school, and I about my life in the States. During a subsequent trip to Ecuador, the family invited me over for dinner. Andrés showed me the original message he'd found that day, somewhat worn but still intact. On a map he had marked the route the bottle took. He estimated that it had floated southeasterly about two hundred miles. Tall and thoughtful, Andrés marveled with me at the circumstances that brought us together. What were the chances of the bottle surviving such a trip, of anyone finding it, of the message inside still being readable, of—of—of—well, we agreed, laughing, it was almost too much to fathom. With the fall of Argentina's military dictatorship, Andrés and his family returned home.

PART FOUR

CHAPTER THIRTY-THREE

PRODUCTION LINE

New York City. "Every time someone moves out of this building," eighty-four-year-old Karl Dorfzaun complained, "a movie company moves in." Dorfzaun was rummaging around the piles of hats that cluttered his office on Broadway near Times Square. Most of the building still housed garment manufacturers and their showrooms. When Karl Dorfzaun first got into the hat business soon after fleeing Germany, his shop was located on Eleventh Street. Among European refugees in the garment trade, his move to the eighth floor of a midtown building symbolized upward mobility.

Shipments arrived from Italy, the Orient, and Ecuador every week. Ecuadoran straw hats come duty free under the Generalized System of Preferences. The GSP, established during the Kennedy administration, waives the import tariff on thousands of items from friendly developing countries. While John Kennedy's penchant for going hatless adversely affected the domestic hat industry, he is credited in Ecuador for making trade with the States more inviting.

The Cuban revolution affected not only the economy in the town of Febres Cordero in Ecuador, at the beginning of the hat trail, but in the office of Karl Dorfzaun in New York as well. "I used to sell beautiful Panamas to Cuba. Montecristis. The men who owned the sugar plantations bought them. They cost five hundred to a thousand dollars apiece. Each one was like silk. That was under Batista."

The market for Ecuadoran straw hats has decreased worldwide of late, Dorfzaun said. "In the early 1970s there was still a demand for Panama hats. In South Africa they bought them for school uniforms. I will sell them there. Germany too. Now mainland China is making imitation Panamas. They're much cheaper, so what am I going to do? I can't push them. I wouldn't work against Ecuador."

Karl Dorfzaun didn't wear a Panama, or, as far as I could tell, any hat at all. I never saw his nephew Kurt in one either. I had asked Ernesto, one of Kurt's sons who helped out around the office during summer vacation, if he ever wore a Panama during the school year in Boston. "*En casa de herrero, cuchillo de palo,*" he replied. In the house of the blacksmith, use a wooden knife. Adriano González didn't wear a straw hat. Nor did anyone in the Ojeda family in Biblián. "We weave the hats for an income, and not for ourselves," Isaura had told me. "We have to make money for our necessities." Victor González, who brought the raw straw from the coast to Biblián—again, no *sombrero de paja toquilla*. Domingo didn't wear one the day we went out to the straw fields, but it seems likely he owned one. On the coast, where no social caste attaches itself to wearing straw hats, they are practically mandatory for constant outdoor labor.

Now, thousands of miles from its homeland, the Panama hat is openly appreciated. Although the hats had already attained some popularity in the United States during the mid-nineteenth century, the first mass exposure of Panamas came during the Spanish-American War, when the United States government ordered fifty thousand Ecuadoran straws for soldiers headed for the Caribbean. The mobster era gave a raffish aura to Panamas. (Hat exporters in Montecristi call the style with the widest brim the Capone.) The hats can be found in the writings of Mark Twain and Graham Greene. They were part of the summer uniform for men during the 1930s and 1940s in the United States, and a race-track necessity in England. No self-respecting movieland detective would be caught without his Panama during the golden era of private-eye films. It became Sydney Greenstreet's trademark, and Charlie Chan's as well. (Both he and his son wore them in *Charlie Chan Goes to Panama*.) Writers such as Tom Wolfe and Garrison Keillor gain an extra measure of élan by wearing Panamas.

Panama hats accentuate the extremes of the people below them and magnify their personalities. In *Lay Bare the Heart*, civil rights leader James Farmer describes a Mississippi prison director during the 1961 freedom rides as "a stereotype of the cotton-belt plantation owner. His middle-aged face and neck were wrinkled, too. Small eyes squinted through gold-rimmed spectacles and white hair peeped from under the Panama on his head." On top of Albert Schweitzer, however, the hat radiated the positive image of a man worth listening to. In the language of fashion, Panamas convey confidence, taste, and achievement.

In New York, United Parcel Service picked up Karl Dorfzaun's unopened shipment of straw-hat bodies from Cuenca, and trucked them to Resistol's plant in Texas. Resistol paid Karl Dorfzaun $43.50 a dozen. The hat bodies that Adriano González bought from Isaura and the other weavers in Biblián for about $.65 were now worth $3.62 each.

Garland, Texas. "There is nothing we could do to improve upon something as classic as the Panama," said Bob Posey, who develops. Resistol's hat line. Posey works a year ahead of time, anticipating fashion trends, merchandising patterns, and availability of raw material. A good corn crop in the Andes can cause a ripple in the straw-hat trade. A Hollywood movie can create a tidal wave.

To most people *Urban Cowboy* was a movie, but in the hat trade it defined the outermost limits of merchandising and manufacturing. "Nobody was prepared for the *Urban Cowboy* explosion," Posey said. "We just couldn't sell enough."

In the straw plant, Tommie Massie was more blunt: "The bigger and uglier the hats we made, the more the public bought them." Such was the demand for western hats made from Ecuadoran straw bodies that the company opened a new plant at Weslaco, Texas, near the Mexican border, and kept it and the home plant in operation day and night. At the height of the boom, Resistol shipped more than one million straw hats in a year, most of them western-style.

"For a long time hats were dead as a fashion item, except for ranchers and cowboys," explained Karl Frankl, who oversees a national sales force of forty-five. "Kennedy's hatlessness influenced young people. Then came the long hair and the flower children, both of which worked against the wearing of hats. Cars at the time were getting lower and lower—it was impossible to get in or out of one with a hat on. The hat industry didn't address these issues, hoping they would just go away. Then *boom! Urban Cowboy* revived a dying industry. Overnight we became the most profitable division within Levi Strauss. The New York cowboy was born—they grubbed at anything. The unknowing consumer bought the cheapest of the cheapest handwoven hats.

"*Urban Cowboy* died because the market was saturated. Men who always wore hats rebelled. They thought that American manufacturers had cheapened authentic American fashion. The real high-quality hat was beyond the reach of the boom. There was always a premium on special hats, like the classic Panama.

"Now we are witnessing a revival in the hat business. The industry is becoming more innovative. The push came with *Raiders of the Lost Ark*, with Indiana Jones sporting that awful-looking fedora. He even wore it to bed! I loved the guy for it. Michael Jackson often has a hat on when he sings. That immediately sends a signal to youth that hats are exciting. The return to short hair makes it easier for people to wear hats. And we have a more conservative type of youth now. More and more young guys going out for job interviews wear hats now. It says something to prospective employers."

Heavy machinery and workers filled Resistol's straw-hat manufacturing plant. The sounds of sewing machines mixed with hydraulic presses and hissing steam. The smell of thick lacquer blended with bleaching formulas and heated straw. Racks full of hats in midproduction rolled down the aisles between work stations. Much of the equipment at the plant is old and no longer made. Some of it is one of a kind, for which company repairmen improvise spare parts. At one end of the plant, which altogether measures about two-thirds the size of a football field, sacks full of straw-hat bodies arrived from Ecuador, the Philippines, China, Japan, Taiwan, and Italy. At the other end, bulky boxes of elegant Panamas went out into the world.

After the hat bodies that came from Cuenca via New York were removed from their cotton bales, the MADE IN ECUADOR stickers were removed. The hats were sorted by size and quality and shipped off to St. Louis, Missouri, for bleaching. The only volume hat bleacher in the country has his operation there, and when he sent Resistol's hats back a few weeks later, they looked a bit lighter, with a completely uniform color. A slight stiffening solution was also added.

At the plant each hat gets a coded Inventory Control Ticket telling the workers at each stop what process that particular hat should undergo. Straw cowboy hats, for example, get drenched in lacquer, dress Panamas get only one coat, and fashion Panamas often get none at all. Like production lines in other industries, the one for finishing straw hats involves numerous operations all in progress simultaneously. Think of the hats' progress through the plant as a river, with tributaries strengthening the flow as they enter it. Plant manager Massie and his bosses synchronize what gets done where by whom, and how often.

The hats from Biblián were softened and stretched; first over a steam table, and then around a metal mold heated to 250 degrees Fahrenheit. A rounder—similar in appearance to a sewing machine through which a hat can be rotated—trimmed the outer brim down to a quarter-inch, just enough to be folded over double-strength for welting. Then an edger, which works about the same way—are you following, Isaura?—cut away the excess from the welting.

Ruth McGee welts hats. "It's like sewing the upper and lower lips together." McGee, who started working for Resistol in 1964, was in her third term as president of Amalgamated Clothing and Textile Workers Union local No. 129-H. "If it wasn't for the union, we wouldn't get any raises." As a right-to-work state, union membership in Texas is not required, but Resistol workers are tied to contracts negotiated between the union and company management. McGee estimated that more than half of the straw plant's 120 hourly workers were members. "If they don't do you right, you've got recourse. For most of us, our pay is tied to production. If your machine breaks down and they don't fix it immediately, you can file a grievance."

Workers at Resistol, who hire on at $3.35 an hour—the 1985 minimum wage—have never gone on strike against the company. With incentive bonuses for exceeding production quotas, some factory hands earn $7.00 and $8.00 an hour. Dolores was earning $5.18 an hour for sewing her quota of 660 sweatbands inside straw hats each day, plus $.79 for each additional dozen she completed daily. She lives in Garland with her husband and three sons. She was in her seventh year at the plant. "If your machine works well," she explained during her half-hour lunch break one day, "you'll do OK. Mine hasn't for the last week or so, and my production's down. I did forty-two dozen hats yesterday. Once I did ninety dozen, but that was years ago." Did she know in what country the straw-hat bodies originated? "I'm not much interested in where they've been before they get to my machine, or where they go once they leave it, as long as Patricia here keeps sending them over. For me it's a job, that's all." Patricia: "I saw some hats in the warehouse once. They said 'Republic of China' on them, so I guess that's where they come from."

There is a healthy mix of black, white, and Mexican employees; well over half the total are women. As the Hispanic with the most seniority on the floor, Julio Melendez, a hat-blocking supervisor, lends a hand to the *novicios*, especially those who speak little or no English. "A lot of the Mexican workers come from San Luis Potosí and Durango. They're all kinfolk—sisters, brothers, uncles. They all know each other. They're used to hard labor and construction, so this is easy. They want to work." I asked him how the workers felt about the imitation Panamas they made for the officials at the Los Angeles Olympics. "People from all over the world watched the games, so there was a little bit of pride in that. Yes, a little bit of pride."

Tommie Massie oversees operations from his office adjoining the plant floor: "We find the Spanish boys, they pick up the knack right away. They're real good at blocking and shaping. I've got one white lady sewing, and two Spanish girls and a black girl. They're all real good."

After being subjected to the rounder, welting, and the edger, the hats went back for one more press in the heated mold to reshape the newly welted outer brims so that they turned upward slightly.

Hats to be lacquered were dunked in a vat, then spin-dried and put on a shelf in a huge rotating oven for a quarter hour. Lacquered or not, all hats were fitted with sweatbands and some with eyelets. One worker lined up each band with the imprint of its destination store, while another inserted a polyester reed through every one. The two ends of the band were linked with a tiny hook, and a little decorative bow was stitched on to each band. Finally they were sewn inside the hats—upside-down, so they could be neatly turned into place.

Outside hatbands were hooked around the crowns, held in place by three pieces of double-stick cellophane tape. The off-white *brisa* fashion Panama from Ecuador was dressed in a blue-and-white band. An adhesive sticker identifying the brand name was placed on a small griddle for a few seconds, then flipped into the center of the inside of each hat. "You have to be pretty accurate," a supervisor explained, "because you only get one chance. You need a good eye." At last, the hats were placed over metal molds to give the inside bands a more finished appearance. Then came inspection, spot check, and packing.

"Occasionally we restructure the location of the work stations for more efficiency," said Rae Crookless in quality control. "If we get a lot of orders for dress hats next year, we'll rearrange operations. The positioning of the workers here depends on fashions out in the marketplace." At full capacity, Resistol turns out three thousand straw hats a day.

The hat bodies from Ecuador, now handsome, finished, and ready for retail sale, had taken eight days to wend their way through the production line. Months earlier hat shops all over the country had learned their price for fashion Panamas from Resistol's sales representatives: $225 a dozen, a five-fold increase over Dorfzaun's price. What started as a shaggy hat body from the Andes for $.65 had become part of mainstream American commerce at a wholesale cost of $18.75.

CHAPTER THIRTY-FOUR

LASTING FRIENDSHIP

When Consolidated Freightways dropped off twenty boxes of Resistol hats at the Western Hat Works in San Diego, Marty Anfangar checked the shipment against the invoice and started stacking the new inventory. Anfangar, in his early forties, is a third-generation hatter. Around the shop he wears a hip-length apron as he moves between his workbench and customers. His grandfather Morris, who came to the United States from Poland, settled in San Diego after serving his new country as an army hat renovator in World War I. He opened his first hat store on Fourth Avenue between A Street and B Street downtown when Warren G. Harding was president. His brother soon opened another store nearby.

The neighborhood thrived with businesses catering to a growing city, especially to maritime commerce and sailors on shore leave. "We did all our own work then," recalled Lew Anfangar, who grew up working in his father's hat shop. "One store would flange the hat, and the other would block it. When I was seven and eight years old I'd walk down the street pushing racks of hats between stores for my father and my uncle. We had a full-time seamstress then. My mother sewed too. We'd put the hats outdoors on the back porch and spin-dry them. We even had a gas-filled dry box."

Lew took over the business after his father's death. Although the store has had five different locations, they've all been within a few blocks of each other in a neighborhood which, during the mid-1980s, was undergoing revitalization. Within one block of Fifth Avenue and E Street, the Western Hat Works location since 1976, you can buy pornography and hardware and eat any of five foreign foods. Public baths and neighborhood poker parlors cater to men who live in nearby flophouses and frequent tawdry burlesque theaters. With the recent round of urban renewal, sidewalk cafés and upscale restaurants have brought suburban clientele to the Gaslamp Quarter, as the neighborhood is known, but police still mop up after barroom brawls, and the after-work sidewalk crowd has a shiftless and menacing character.

"There was a time when you could walk around downtown at any hour without fear of being mugged," Marty said between customers. "That isn't so anymore. The scum of the earth come in now and then. We used to be open until six o'clock. Now we're out of here every day at five." The door buzzer sounded, announcing the entrance of another customer. Marty went to wait on him, and Lew continued: "He doesn't allow anyone to give me any back talk. One time a guy came in acting a little gruff. Marty chased after him. I leapt on him to keep him back, and he ran out of the store with me on his back." He looked across the store at his son. "I wish he'd smile more."

When hats were part of every man's apparel, San Diego boasted seven different hat-renovating establishments. Western Hat Works is the only one left. The strength of its reputation far outweighs that of the neighborhood, and hat buyers from all over the metropolitan area—including Tijuana, Mexico—regularly find their way to the store. Besides the usual assortment of caps and street and western hats, the Anfangars stock hats from Czechoslovakia, South Africa, and England. They can oblige the rare customer who asks for a silk collapsible opera hat from Austria. A steady stream of drill instructors from the Marine Corps Recruitment Depot drop off their brown Smokey the Bear hats for reshaping and cleaning.

The store's upper two floors carry stock ready to move downstairs when space becomes available. The back of the third floor holds old, forgotten hats that look like they'd be resplendent with a good dusting. "I hate doing inventory in that place," said Lyle Hatch, an old friend and Resistol's California salesman for many years. "I'm always afraid all those boxes will come tumbling down on me." Including its upstairs stock, Western Hat Works carries five thousand hats.

"For a long time," Lew reflected, "the Panama was the God of the industry. It was a hat of distinction. Seamen who'd sailed from Ecuadoran ports used to come in and sell them to us. Personally, I prefer the Shantung," the imitation Panama from the Orient. "It wears better."

A week earlier, a fellow had walked in hoping to sell a Panama to Western Hat Works. Marty recognized it as a Montecristi *fino*. "The guy wanted eighty dollars for it. I bought it right away." He lifted his prize from its balsa-wood cradle. In the marketplace of superior-grade Panamas, it was worth far more than eighty dollars. "In fact, it's so good I'm not even sure I want to sell it. As for regular straws, you'll always find people who'll pay good money for a Panama when they could get a Shantung for less. The Panama is more durable."

On his way to work one morning from his home in the suburbs, Ray Stansbury was struck by the coming of spring. For the forty-seven-year-old pest-control company executive, that meant one thing: time to buy a new Panama hat. He didn't know where the hats were made, but for years he had admired their workmanship. The previous weekend he'd taken an old Panama out of the closet of his home in Encinitas and worn it to Old Town. Strangers had complimented him and asked where he got it.

Growing up on a ranch in Oklahoma, Stansbury had worn a straw hat since he was five years old. "We'd go to town to get a new one every summer. They'd be shapeless, so to soften them up for shaping we'd toss them in the horse tank." He has not forgotten how to reshape a hat; he still does it at home. "A couple of weekends ago I dropped my fishing hat in the lake. Damn near lost it. I had to reshape it. The first thing you do is give it a real soaking. Then you lay it flat on the work-shop table and put a plywood ring around it. I use one with a hole in it just big enough for the hat to fit through. When it dries to the point where it's just damp, you can shape it with your hands any way you want. I put mine on my head so when it's completely dry and stiffens, the crown will fit perfectly. These newer hats with thinner straw, I spray them with some starch from my wife's ironing board. To clean them, I soak them in light detergent, then I brush them."

Pictures and drawings of John Wayne fill the wall of Stansbury's den at home. A half-dozen more line his office at work. "As the years go by, you don't give up something you enjoy. My brother-in-law and I like to find hat shops whenever we go out of town. We buy straw hats and give them to each other or to friends. You know, a man looks so different in a hat. To give another man a hat, well—there's something about it that creates a bond. It's a lasting friendship."

The day Ray Stansbury decided a new Panama was in order, he dropped in at Western Hat Works during his lunch hour. He had bought hats there before and thought they had the best selection in town. He looked at a few Shantungs, tried on a couple of natural straws, and decided on a Panama, *brisa* style. A blue-and-white band circled the off-white body. Sales clerk Alicia Del Rio rang it up: $35, plus $2.10 state sales tax.

I told Ray a little of the story behind the hat and how much the weavers in the Andes earned. "Really?" he said. "That's some markup." Instead of putting his new Panama hat in a box or a bag, he wore it out the door and then for the rest of the day.

ACKNOWLEDGMENTS

For a book that deals with life along the equator, I benefited by sound advice from people as far north as the Arctic Circle and as far south as Santiago, Chile. Suggestions came in the form of books to read, ideas to consider, and friends to meet. Seasoned travelers recommended towns to visit and those to avoid; experienced translators gave nuance in English to poems in Spanish.

The people of Ecuador, whether on the coast, in the Andes, or in the jungle, went far out of their way to show me their culture. They opened their doors and shared their knowledge; to all of them I am grateful. I remember them well, and at one stop on the trail found that they remembered me, too. I had spent some time in the wilderness with the men who harvest the straw from which Panama hats are woven. One year later I returned to the same place, and reintroduced myself. "I came here a year ago," I told them. "Perhaps you recall me from then."

"Of course we remember you," a man replied. "You were the last one to visit us."

For their equatorial hospitality, John and Sam Miller deserve special gratitude, along with Miriam González and John Daane, and Shari Villarosa. To the following friends—both new and old—whose counsel and support kept me on the trail, a tip of the Panama and *un abrazo*: Dan Anderson, Joe Brenner, Kathryn Coe, Olga Fisch, Kurt Dorfzaun, Michael Earney, Enrique Grosse-Luemern, Charles W. Grover, John and Mary Lou Hay, Mercedes Herrera Ayamar, Lynn Hirschkind, Robert Houston, Anita Hughes, Milton Johnson, Charles A. Miller, Nick Mills, Jacqueline de Munizaga, Boyd Nicholl and Laurie Kintzele, J. Enrique Ojeda, María Olano, Fabián Peñaherrera, Valerina Quintana, Osvaldo Viteri, Ion Youman, Stefan Schinzinger, Martha Sowerwine, Moritz Thomsen, and Donna Waldman.

Appreciation is also due the hat companies in Ecuador and the United States. They opened their factories and their ledgers to me without once looking over my shoulder to see what I was doing.

—T.M.

BIBLIOGRAPHY

Acosta-Solis, M., et al. *Ecuador in the Shadow of the Volcanoes.* Quito: Ediciones Libri Mundi, 1981.

Agee, Philip. *Inside the Company: CIA Diary.* New York: Bantam, 1976.

Aguilar de Tamariz, María Leonor. *La Industria de los Sombreros de Paja Toquilla.* Cuenca: Master's thesis, 1981.

Alboñez, Victor Manuel. *Cuenca y Su Industria de Tejidos de Sombreros de Paja Toquilla.* Cuenca: Self-published, 1949.

Anhalzer, Jorge and Ramiro Navarrete. *Por los Andes del Ecuador.* Quito: Ediciones Campoabierto, 1983.

Bemelmans, Ludwig. *The Donkey Inside.* New York: Viking, 1941.

Blomberg, Rolf. *Ecuador: Andean Mosaic.* Stockholm: H. Gerber, 1952.

Brandi, John. *Andean Town Circa 1980.* Guadalupita, N.Mex.: Tooth of Time Press, 1978.

———, ed. *Chimborazo—Life on the Haciendas of Highland Ecuador.* Rooseveltown, N.Y.: Akwesasne Notes, 1976.

———. *Diary from a Journey to the Middle of the World.* Berkeley, Calif.: The Figures, 1979.

———. *Narrowgauge to Riobamba.* Santa Barbara, Calif.: Christopher's Books, 1975.

Brownrigg, Leslie Ann. *The "Nobles" of Cuenca: The Agrarian Elite of Southern Ecuador.* New York: Ph.D. dissertation, Columbia University, 1972.

Cajamarca Lema, Sofía. "Artesanía del Sombrero de Paja Toquilla en El Cantón de Biblián, Provincia de Cañar." Biblián: unpublished monograph, 1984.

Carvalho-Neto, Paulo de. *Diccionario del Folklore Ecuatoriano.* Quito: Casa de la Cultura Ecuatoriana, 1964.

Centro Interamericano de Artesanías y Artes Populares. *Sombreros de Paja Toquilla.* Cuenca: CIDAP, 1982.

Church, George Earl. *A Report upon Ecuador.* Washington, D.C.: Government Printing Office, 1882.

Cordova, Carlos J. *Vocabulario Usado en el Industria del Tejido del Sombrero de Paja Toquilla*. Cuenca: Revista del Instituto Azuayo de Folklore, 1973.

Cuesta y Cuesta, Alfonso. *Los Hijos*. Caracas: Monte Avila Editores C. A., 1969.

Curtis, William Eleroy. *Between the Andes and the Ocean*. Chicago: Herbert S. Stone & Co., 1920.

DellaPergola, Sergio. "Population Trends of Latin American Jewry." Jerusalem: Unpublished monograph, 1984.

Domínguez O., M. Ernesto. *Sombreros de Paja Toquilla*. Cuenca: Camara de Comercio de Cuenca, 1969.

El Ecuador Visto Por Los Extranjeros (Viajeros de los Siglos XVIII y XIX). Puebla, Mexico: Biblioteca Ecuatoriana Minima, 1960.

Elkin, Judith Laikin. *Jews of the Latin American Republics*. Chapel Hill, N.C.: University of North Carolina Press, 1980.

Exportadores de Sombreros de Paja Toquilla. *El Problema del Toquilla Inventado por Luis Monsalve Pozo*. Cuenca: Self-published, 1953.

Franck, Harry A. *Vagabonding Down the Andes*. New York: Grosset & Dunlap, 1917.

Goding, Frederic Webster. *A Brief History of the American Consulate General at Guayaquil, Ecuador*. Livermore Falls, Maine: Self-published, 1920.

Handelman, Howard. "Ecuadorian Agrarian Reform: The Politics of Limited Change." Hanover, N.H.: American Universities Field Staff Reports, No. 49, 1980.

Hassaurek, Friedrich. *Four Years Among the Ecuadorians*. Carbondale, Ill.: Southern Illinois University Press, 1967.

Hecht, Ben. *To Quito and Back*. New York: Covici, Friede, 1937.

Hirschkind, Lynn. *On Conforming in Cuenca*. Madison, Wisc.: Ph.D. dissertation, University of Wisconsin, 1981.

Humboldt, Alexander von. *Personal Narrative of Travels to the Equinoctial Regions of America During the Years 1799–1804*, trans. Helen Williams. Philadelphia: M. Carey, 1815.

Hurtado, Oswaldo. *Political Power in Ecuador*, trans. Nick D. Mills. Albuquerque, N.Mex.: University of New Mexico Press, 1980.

Icaza, Jorge. *The Villagers (Huasipungo)*, trans. Bernard M. Dulsey. Carbondale, Ill.: Southern Illinois University Press, 1964.

Inwards, Harry. *Straw Hats: Their History and Manufacture*. London: Sir I. Pitman and Sons, Ltd., 1922.

Kalechofsky, Roberta, ed. *An Anthology of Latin American Jewish Writers*. Marblehead, Mass.: Micah Publications, 1980.

Lernoux, Penny. *Cry of the People*. Garden City, N.Y.: Doubleday, 1980.

Lupsha, Peter A. "Narcotics Politics and Policy: The Changing Case of Ecuador." Albuquerque, N.Mex.: Unpublished monograph, 1985.

Lydenberg, Harry Miller. *Crossing the Line: Tales of the Ceremony During Four Centuries*. New York: New York Public Library, 1957.

Marcoy, Paul (Laurent Saint-Criq). *Travels in South America*. London: Blackie & Son, 1875.

Mata, G. H. Juan Cuenca: *Biografía del Pueblo Sombrerero*. Cuenca: Biblioteca Cenit, 1978.

Matthiessen, Peter. *At Play in the Fields of the Lord*. New York: Bantam, 1976.

Meisch, Lynn. *A Traveler's Guide to El Dorado and the Inca Empire*. New York: Penguin, 1980.

Michaux, Henri. *Ecuador: A Travel Journal*, trans. Robin Magowan. Seattle: University of Washington Press, 1970.

Monsalve Pozo, Luis. *El Sombrero de Paja Toquilla—Azuaya*. Cuenca: Anales de la Universidad de Cuenca, abril-junio 1953.

Muratorio, Ricardo. *A Feast of Color: Corpus Christi Dance Costumes of Ecuador*. Washington, D.C.: Smithsonian Institution Press, 1981.

Orton, James. *The Andes and the Amazon*. New York: Harper & Bros., 1876.

Paine, Albert Bigelow. *Th. Nast: His Period and His Pictures*. New York: Harper & Brothers, 1904.

Reyes, Oscar Efrén. *Breve Historia General del Ecuador* (3 vols.). Quito: Publisher unknown, 1966.

Rodman, Selden. *South America of the Poets*. New York: Hawthorn Books, 1970.

Rothchild, John, ed. *Latin America Yesterday and Today*. New York: Bantam, 1973.

Sandberg, Harry O. *The Jews of Latin America*. Philadelphia: The Jewish Publishing Society of America, 1917.

Santovenía, Emeterio S. *Eloy Alfaro of Ecuador*. Havana: Academy of History of Cuba, 1935.

Thomsen, Moritz. *The Farm on the River of Emeralds*. New York: Houghton Mifflin, 1978.

————. *Living Poor: A Peace Corps Chronicle*. Seattle: University of Washington Press, 1969.

Traven, B. *The Night Visitor and Other Stories*. London: Allison & Busby, 1983.

Twain, Mark (Samuel L. Clemens). *Following the Equator: A Journey Around the World* (2 vols.). New York: Harper & Brothers, 1897.

de Ulloa, Antonio. *A Voyage to South America*, trans. John Adams. Boston: Milford House, 1972.

U.S. Consulate, Guayaquil. *Despatches from United States Consuls in Guayaquil, Ecuador, 1826–1906*. Washington, D.C.: National Archives (microfilm).

von Hagen, Victor W. *Ecuador and the Galápagos Islands*. Norman, Okla.: University of Oklahoma Press, 1949.

————. *Highway of the Sun*. New York: Duell, Sloan and Pearce, 1955.

Vintimilla, Julio Carpio. *Cuenca—Su Geografía Urbana*. Cuenca: López Monsalve Editores, 1979.

Waldman, Donna. *Ecuador: A History*. Quito: Unpublished manuscript, 1982.

Whitten, Norman E., Jr. *Cultural Transformations and Ethnicity in Modern Ecuador*. Urbana, Ill.: University of Illinois Press, 1981.

Whymper, Edward. *Travels Amongst the Great Andes of the Equator*. New York: Charles Scribner's Sons, 1892.

Wolf, Theodore. *Geology and Geography of Ecuador*, trans. James W. Flanagan. Toronto: Grand and Toy, 1933.

Wood, Bryce. *Aggression and History: The Case of Ecuador and Peru*. Ann Arbor, Mich.: Published for the Institute of Latin American Studies, Columbia University, by University Microfilms, International, 1978.

Zahm, John Augustine (H. J. Mozans). *Along the Andes and Down the Amazon*. New York: D. Appleton and Co., 1911.

INDEX

ABOUT THE AUTHOR

Tom Miller's eleven books include *Trading with the Enemy*, *On the Border*, *Revenge of the Saguaro*, and, most recently, *Cuba, Hot and Cold*. His articles on Latin America and the American Southwest have appeared in *Smithsonian*, *LIFE*, the *New York Times*, and *Rolling Stone*, among other magazines. The capital of Ecuador has proclaimed Miller "Un Huésped Illustre de Quito" for his literary contribution to the country, especially *The Panama Hat Trail*. He lives in Tucson, Arizona, where he is affiliated with the Latin American Studies Center at the University of Arizona.